"Therefore encourage one another and build each other up, just as in fact you are doing."
**1 Thessalonians 5:11**

# THE ENCOURAGER

**DOT GOLDIE**

Little Red Rocking Chair Publishing
www.littleredrockingchair.com

# The Encourager

Copyright © 2014 by Dot Goldie

Cover and Book Design by: Maritza Cosano

All rights reserved. No part of this book may be reproduced in any form by any electronic or mechanical means, including photocopying, recording, or information storage and retrieval without permission in writing from the author.

ISBN-13: 978-0-692-25074-7

Send your letters to the publisher,
Little Red Rocking Chair Publishing
www.LittleRedRockingChair/Home.com
Email: Maritza@littleredrockingchair.com

Write to the author at:
dot@dotgoldie.com

Printed in U.S.A

## Dedication

*To my darling husband and best friend Jim,
And to my wonderful children
Derek, Alan and Sharon,
And all my beautiful grandchildren
Ryan, Marli, Austin, Madison, Christopher,
Emily, Ross and Haley*

# Introduction

God's Word is faithful and true. That's the hope that you and I have. I pray that as you read this book, your heart will be encouraged as you realize that *"Jesus Christ is the same yesterday and today and forever."*

I wholeheartedly believe our faith leads us, charting the course of our lives, most especially when we are traveling through hard times. Our faith in Jesus causes us to see life through a different set of lenses. It propels us to hope in the things not seen and boldly believe in the power of God's mighty and victorious right hand. Our love for Him influences us to love and encourage others, and to depend on Him for everything. Indeed, very few people realize that we have the ability to impact the lives of others by simply praying for them and believing we are the messengers God uses to deliver His blessings.

The short stories you are about to read in the next pages of this book are a testament of this truth. I pray that my words will encourage you, and that His Word might strengthen you, as it has done for me and countless others many times. The Lord has always come to my rescue in my times of need and He will do the same for you, beloved.

# "WRITE A BOOK!"

## *Lord, Me?*

Over the years, many people from all walks of life have said to me, "You should write a book!" Often I'd begin to write something then I'd get interrupted or I'd just stop! Maybe it was my insecurities, or perhaps it was the enemy whispering into my ear, trying to control me and keeping me from fulfilling God's destiny for my life. Each time that the thought of writing a book came to my mind, I would ignore it.

I understand completely that choosing to do something that you've never tried is not always easy. But one of the best exercises you can try is… no, it's not spinning or Pilates, it is actually controlling your thoughts. This is a lifetime journey, and I'll tell you more about it and encourage you in yours, as this book unfolds.

As time passed, again someone would say, "Dot, you should write a book!" But I would always take fright and

## The Encourager

think, I don't know where to begin. I don't know how to type or use a computer.

The battle in my mind would continue, not realizing that the mind is a battlefield and I was becoming a victim of my own thoughts. The biggest challenge we face is our own minds, because we have an enemy that is constantly harassing us, deceiving us and threatening our creative ideas. God's Word tells us to guard our minds from the lies the enemy tells us, which often results in wrong thinking.

And that's exactly where I was at, until one day my friend Bill Gilvear told me how he wrote his book. He got a tape recorder and spoke into it and got someone else to type it out for him. So, my darling husband Jim bought me a little recorder to speak into. *But, could I do that?* No! I felt awkward talking into a machine. Time passed and again more people would say, "Dot, write a book. It would encourage so many people!"

*Lord, is that you speaking through these people?* By now I began to wonder. And then His voice got louder in my mind, and thoughts of His goodness in my life began to surface in the form of stories—my relationship with Him, the

### **Dot Goldie**

wonders He had done in my life and in the lives of people I had met in all my travels and walks of life. And that's when I started thinking about you, my beloved reader.

The goal of this book is not simply to encourage you and fill your minds with stories that you can store away somewhere in your mind. My hope is that my words change your life so that then you can do the same for others. Don't you see? It's the model Jesus left us. His Father sent Him to tell His story, so that others would believe and have eternal life.

My story is not that grand and could never, ever be compared to the *Greatest Story Ever Told*, but the Lord has done miracles in my life for a very good reason—so that I would share them with you, and you would believe He could do the same for you. For God doesn't play favorites. He loves us all the same—and hears us when we call upon His name.

## The Encourager

# THE GIFT CERTIFICATE

My life verse is Philippians 4:19, which says, *"My God shall supply all your needs from His riches in glory through Christ Jesus."* And it's true! God has been the supplier of all my needs.

Times were difficult for us financially when my husband Jim and I came to America. Jim's work was not always steady and with three children to feed and clothe, money was very tight. One night after our evening meal, I informed the family that our refrigerator was empty. We had no money until Jim's next payday.

My husband used to tell me I could make a meal out of nothing. But on this fine day, I proved him wrong.

"All we have is ice cubes and one solitary orange!" I told him and everyone just sat at the table in unbelief. "Let's pray, for God is our 'Jehovah Jira,'" I said, trusting our provider. So, we all prayed. Just as I was about to clear away the dishes, a knock came to the door. I got up and answered it. It was a young man from our church.

"Hi George, what can I do for you?" I said with a smile. "Come on in!" The young man looked at me and then at the rest of the family.

"It's not what you can do for me, but what I can do for you!" He said. "My wife Linda and I were praying last night and the Lord put you on our hearts to pray for you, and for some reason we both were led to give you this."

I looked at him and said, "What is this?"

"Open it," he said, rushing on almost apologetically for his kind gesture. "I don't know why we were to do this, and I hope you won't be offended."

I proceeded to open the envelope and inside was a gift certificate for Publix Supermarket in the amount of $80, more than enough to feed us until Jim's next payday! When we related our predicament to George, he was overcome with emotion and was so happy that he and Linda had been obedient to the prompting of the Holy Spirit.

Previously to George's visit that evening, Jim and I had prayed for George and his little family. He and Linda had four boys and they didn't have much either. One of their boys was

## The Encourager

sick and we had prayed for him, and the Lord healed him.

"We were thanking the Lord for His mercy and healing and that's when God spoke to us about your need," explained George.

We were utterly amazed at the Lord's awesome provision, and so we praised Him together and cried tears of joy when George left.

## THE TWO MOMS

Second grade is the best! I love second graders and their moms. Two in particular come to mind. Mrs. Carson, Michael's mom and Dr. Tucker, Chris's mom. These two women have been an inspiration to me to write this book.

One day after school both ladies were staying behind to help Mrs. Keogler, second grade teacher. I was her aide and was about to start grading some papers for her, when I overheard the ladies discussing some things that were bothering them. I offered some counsel, as I have been trained as a biblical counselor at my wonderful church, Calvary Chapel Fort Lauderdale.

I shared God's Word with them, as well as some of my testimony of what God has done in my life. Before I knew it, two hours had passed and I never got to grade the papers for Mrs. Keogler. She didn't mind, though. She was actually happy that I'd helped two of her moms.

"We need the older women to teach us younger

## The Encourager

moms how to walk in the faith and apply God's Word to our daily lives," said Mrs. Carson.

"Would you have a Bible study some night that we could come and be taught?" Asked Dr. Tucker.

"I would love to," I said. "But at present I am already committed to a group at my church and between that and church commitments I can't do it right then." That was my answer, but God obviously had something else in mind.

From time to time, whenever I'd see them at school, I would stop and pray with them and talk about things that were happening in their lives. And so, God used these little moments to touch and change our lives.

Life is precious and the older we get the more we realize that. The society we live in today is filled with long and "to-do" lists and people who don't have time to talk, really talk with the person next to them. Sure, there's technology that makes it easier each day to talk to anyone in the world at any given time, and yet, we don't even have two minutes to share God's Word with a friend or someone who needs to hear a kind word of encouragement. No wonder people, especially young Christian women, are stressed out! In Titus

2, older women are instructed to teach the younger women the following seven things:

- To love their husbands
- To love their children
- To be discreet
- To be chaste
- To be homemakers
- To be good
- To be obedient to their husbands

This is the kind of teaching that older women should be sharing with younger women today, so that they may not flounder, but know where to turn to (Hint: Jesus) and how to make wise decisions in their lives. We often avoid many of these topics. Could it be that our modern culture has either rejected many of these virtues, or at least forgotten them?

Life is too short to waste our days without sharing God's wisdom with others. Anything that God has given us, He expects us to extend to others. If He gives us wisdom, we should share it. If it's a talent, let's pass it on. If He encourages us, we should encourage others. That should be our goal. For encouragement comes from the Lord, and "discouragement" comes from the enemy. Don't allow him to deceive you with an "I can't," mentality. In contrast, say to yourself, "I can!" And

## The Encourager

let the power of the Holy Spirit change your life and that of others.

For my older women sisters, remember the admonition the Apostle Paul gave to us: be reverent, not slanderers, not given to much wine, and teachers of good things. Let's be encouraged to teach those "good things" that we've learned to younger women.

To younger women: be teachable. Seek out godly older women and listen and learn what they have to say. Don't get angry or defensive when they speak the truth, or consider their advice "outdated" or their teaching antiquated. Instead, think and do what Proverbs 22:17 says, *"Incline your ear and hear the words of the wise, and apply your heart to my knowledge."*

## WRITE IT DOWN

Many people fail to do what it is their desire to do for lack of confidence. Sometimes we need each other to push one another. In my case, it was those two lovely moms from second grade who encouraged me to begin writing this book.

They bought me books on "How to write," "How to get Started," and other examples of what to do next. But like the recorder, I started to read, then lost interest. Still, always on the back of my mind were the voices and faces of these two moms. Waiting, asking, encouraging me to write "the book."

During one particular summer, I began to pray for inspiration. I had time alone away from the routine of school, the grandchildren, and my beloved Jim, who was at work all day. It was only Molly, my little white Westie, and me. She often lives at my feet, and when I write, she only moves when I do, or if she needs to go outside to do her business.

That day, I was writing and thinking of the two moms, and I hoped they would be happy with the outcome of all this

## The Encourager

writing, because it was them who stirred up the fire that the Lord had placed in my heart back in 1981!

"Write down what I tell you," He'd said, but the procrastinator that I am, I hadn't done anything. I remember when it happened. I was reading my Bible and praying about our coming to America. Jim was already in Florida, when God began to really speak to my heart. He gave me many Scriptures to encourage me, but let me start from the beginning, as stories often do.

While we were living in Scotland, we attended a conference. We got there late. The theater, where the speaker was addressing the assembly, was filled to capacity. Jim found me a single seat at the back of the theater hall, then went out to the overflow room to listen and watch on the monitor that was set up to accommodate the surplus of people at the conference.

The evening was full of missionaries sharing their testimonies. It was all very exciting to me and as each one spoke, my heart beat loudly, so much that I thought I was going to have a heart attack. It was a heart attack, but not the kind you think! It was God knocking on the door of my heart, asking me to go for Him. The sound of this simple word shook my body until it pierced my soul.

By the time the last speaker got up and made an "altar call" for those wishing to "Serve the Lord" to come forward, it felt like my heart wanted to come out of my chest. I wasn't mentally prepared for this challenge, and so, I sat in my seat, making all sorts of excuses why not to go forward.

*I'm way up here in the back, I'm in the middle of a long row, Jim won't understand if I go forward,* I told myself.

And then without thinking, I told the Lord, "I love Jim, but I love You and want what You want."

All these things were rushing through my mind when all of a sudden the voice of the speaker broke through the noise in my head and the deep whispers in my heart. "If you are in the middle of a row, the folks beside you won't mind you getting up and coming forth," I heard him say. My heart leapt again and before I knew it, I began the long walk down the aisle.

As I walked I was praying up a storm saying, "Please Lord, let Jim understand what I'm doing. I love him, but I love You more! He's the breadwinner, let him know what

## The Encourager

You're doing in my life." Finally, I reached the stage area where counselors were standing holding out packets in a big envelope. The speaker prayed for those of us who came forward and invited us to come to a meeting the following morning. I was both excited and anxious at the same time, as I was now to face Jim with what I'd just done.

Holding on to my envelope I prayed again as I made my way out to meet Jim at our appointed meeting place. Can you imagine the expression on my face and his when we met each other?

Here I was all anxious and worried about what he would say, little did I know that Jim had gone forward in the overflow room when he heard the call to full time ministry too! There he was, standing with envelope in hand and all anxious looking, hoping I would understand what he had done in going forward.

Jim had felt the same as I did, telling the Lord the same things I had, about his preoccupation of being the breadwinner in the family. God had touched us both, and had told both to "Go!" We both were ecstatic. We jumped up and down, and then went to get our kids from the nursery and youth group, got them settled in bed and then went to find our minister, who also was at the conference. He confirmed our move that God was calling us to serve Him together as a couple.

*But, where?*

That was the question.

That would hopefully be answered at the next morning at the missionary meeting. We could hardly sleep that night. *What would the morning hold for us?* Only God knew the answer to that!

## THE NEXT MORNING

Jim and I were up early and eager to find out what God's plan for our lives would be. We got our children off to their classes and then headed off to the theater, where we were to meet the missionaries. Once we got there, we both went around all the tables and talked with several of the ministries, but none seemed to fit us both, and we truly believed God wanted us both to be serving Him together as a team.

We decided to take some time alone in a corner of the room and just pray this thing through, and find exactly what it was that God intended for our lives. It didn't take long. We noticed a girl at an information desk and decided to tell her our dilemma. After hearing our story of how God called us the night before, she told us of a Children's Home that needed house parents.

That was all we needed to hear and it was as though a light went on, and "Click" our hearts raced at the thought of us doing something like this, together. After all, we had no training in anything other than Jim being a carpenter and I, being a mom, but we were parents!

A meeting was set up for us to talk with Alan Vincent who was the accountant for Mr. Fegan's Home. We were so excited at the prospect of working full time for the Lord.

The meeting went well and we had the opportunity to also meet with a wonderful couple Ann and Martin Granger, an English couple who were serving as house parents at the time in one of the eight homes that was called Mr. Fegan's Homes throughout the south of England.

Ann and Martin did not paint a pretty picture for us, but the more they told us, the more we wanted to be a part of it all. The stories of how difficult the children were or the "work" of cleaning toilets, etc. just filled us with enthusiasm and a desire of becoming house parents.

We were overwhelmed.

*Could this actually be happening to us?*

*God calling us to serve Him?*

Have you ever heard the "Bang!" of a car backfiring, as we called it in Scotland? Well, that's what happened after

## The Encourager

our return home from that conference. We were all fired up, ready to go, and then the "big let down" or backfiring.

Fegan's Home had no openings at present, but they were trying to sell some property in order to purchase another home. They asked us to keep in touch with them and they would keep us up to date with what was going on as far as buying a new facility.

Jim and I were deflated to say the least. We thought God called us so we must be ready. *What was the deal, Lord?* I wondered. Soon God began to show us it was not our plans but His, that was the deal. Some close friends at our church had told us The Church of Scotland had Children's Homes.

"There's no need for you to go to England when there is a need here in Scotland," they said. So, the Assistant Minister, Mr. Trimble, made an appointment for us to interview with the people at George St. Edinburgh, the headquarters for the Church of Scotland.

I remember the day well. It was about 4pm, the rain was pouring down. The sky was dark and the air cold. We went upstairs to the reception area. It was a bleak looking room. I felt cold; the place was quiet and empty of anything

## Dot Goldie

like life. A solemn woman met us, handed us some papers, told us to read the rules, and then a committee would interview us. Jim and I sat and looked at each other, glanced at the RULES and both of us came to the same conclusion.

*This was not for us.*

We felt called by God to serve Him, not do a job for the Church of Scotland, which clearly was looking for employees. They were not concerned that God's call was on our lives, so we left. We did not interview with the committee, and told the lady we were not the ones for the job. We ran back to our car and drove to a nearby fish and chip shop and got our dinner to go, then drove up to Arthur's Seat overlooking Auld Reekie (Edinburgh) on the bleakest night ever.

We ate our fish and chips and drank our Irn Bru (soda) and talked things out together, and prayed to our Heavenly Father about where we should go from there.

It was not long before we got our answer.

God always hears us and knows our hearts' desire to serve Him. My friend Betty Miller was a social worker with the children's department. She told us of a campaign that

## The Encourager

was underway throughout Scotland for foster parents, and wanted to know if we would we would consider being a part of this program, and foster some of the children in need.

"Short term only," she said.

We prayed about it and before we knew it, we had three new family members.

*Now what?* Six children and two bedrooms. Something's got to change.

I was still in touch with Fegan's Home, but nothing was moving there so we decided we needed something bigger if we were going to foster children. We looked around and found a house not far from where we lived in Dalkeith. It had three bedrooms, two bathrooms, an eat-in kitchen, and a big living room, with plenty of room for the kids to play in.

We fostered kids "short term" until their families could get their lives straightened out, then the children would return to their parents.

This was an eye opener for us as parents, because we never really knew what some people go through in their lives. We were a happy little family of five: mom and dad, two handsome boys, and a beautiful little girl. Life for us was just fine, and holidays were even better by the seaside every summer at our caravan in North Berwick.

Jim worked steadily and I was a housewife. We didn't have any money to talk of, but we had a nice rental home, and a nice car. We had a great church and good friends, and we never had trouble with police or social workers or other people trying to take our kids away from us. We were just a nice and quiet contented church-going, little family until, we fostered other children.

All of a sudden, we had to deal with lice infested hair, which I was not used to, but learned quickly to get rid of the pests. Every night, everyone got their head looked at, including Jim, who hardly had any hair, but what he did have got scrutinized.

We also had to deal with parents who were at war with one another, and the police were called in. Like in the case of the little girl whose grandparents were torn up because of the breakups in the family, and needed to see their grandchild before she was taken away to the home for deaf children.

## The Encourager

Then there was little Maria. She was the same age as my own little girl Sharon. Only Maria had a big bloated tummy from malnutrition. Maria was a little spitfire. She had been in several homes before coming to us. She wanted to rule the roost until I put my foot down.

"You have to learn some new behavior if you're going to be in our family," I told her. It was tough at first but she eventually calmed down and settled in as part of the Goldie clan.

My friend Sheila Galloway was a dressmaker and she made some beautiful outfits for both Sharon and Maria. They looked like twins. This however did not last.

Soon Maria's mom came for her to take her away to London to live with her and her boyfriend. I was not ready for what happened next.

All my neighbors came out to say goodbye to Maria, who once was a fireball and didn't want anything to do with us, and was now crying and holding out her arms to me saying, "Mommy, Mommy... let me stay."

I was a mess.

The social worker had warned me this day was

coming, but I never realized how hard it would be to part with her. The mother and boyfriend thanked me and got in the car and left. All the neighbors were crying.

Six months later, I heard from my friend Betty that Maria had died. Her body was found abandoned in a shop front somewhere in London. I've never gotten over that to this day.

I don't know what happened or how. It was a sad time in my life. I know this, though. God knows. All this was preparation for what He was calling us.

## THE CALL

One day I was cleaning out some drawers in my living room cabinet and I came across a letter I had begun to write to Fegan's House. I had started to tell them of my move and of our fostering children.

I stopped what I was doing and finished the letter, then popped it in the mail. I had asked if there had been any progress made with the properties, etc. and that we were still very much interested in serving as house parents whenever a position became available.

Three days later, I got a reply from Fegan's House saying they had been trying to get in touch with us but the letters were being returned "Gone Away." They were delighted that we had made contact again and wanted us to come for an interview down in London at their head office.

*What a surprise!* I was so excited. I couldn't wait for Jim to come home from work to tell him the good news. Jim was as nervous and excited as I was. We called our little Bible study group Peter, Margaret Waugh, Sheila, Hamish and Margot McRae and the Trimbles, and prayed.

Hamish gave us some good advice: "Fly down to London, so you will be fresh for the interview and then get the bus back."

We were concerned about finances and wanted to be good stewards of what we had, even though Fegan's House had said they would reimburse us for our expenses.

We prayed, "Lord, we don't want to take money from them as they depend on others for their needs." If this was God's will for us, He would provide for us. So we set off for London. The Trimbles took the two boys, and Peter and Margaret, who are Sharon's Godparents, took her.

So all was a go! Jim and I were both overjoyed at the thought of us being called by God. Our heads were literally in the clouds as we flew to London. We found the address of the lawyers office, which we thought was Fegan's headquarters, but it was the office of one of the House Committee members. He was the chairman of Fegan's Home. We entered a room where two other couples were seated

## The Encourager

and sat next to them. Just as we got seated, Alan Vincent came out to greet us.

"We will see you shortly," he said and smiled, as he escorted one of the other couples into the next room. For a moment all was silent. Then I broke the silence and turned to the woman next to me.

"We are here for the position of house parents," I said.

"So are we!" She said with a Scottish accent. My heart sank. Hamish and Peter and all our Bible study group had said to us, "They wouldn't be asking you to go all that long way and not give you the position and offer to pay your way too!"

Well, I believed that too, but right here in front of me was Linda and Ian Williamson, a young Scottish couple, who not only wanted to be house parents, but also were the children of missionaries, and they had been on the mission field helping their parents. My hope sank. *What were our chances?* Jim and I were the only Christians in our family.

Soon Alan reappeared and invited the Williamsons into the other room. He gave us a smile and said, "We'll be with you soon." The other couple must have left from another door because we never saw them come out. It seemed like hours as we sat in that waiting room. Jim and I were going over in our minds what God was going to do. We really thought because we came from Scotland we would get picked, but Linda and Ian were from Scotland too, so that really threw us for a loop. Still, we were here fresh off the plane and ready for whatever God had in store for us.

Alan appeared at the door again and smiled and escorted us into the room. There they were. The Committee. Twelve people, English to the core, sitting around a huge conference table, looking at us like we were peasants ready to see the Queen. Alan introduced us as Mr. and Mrs. Goldie. Everyone smiled, and then Sir Arthur spoke.

"Welcome," he said. "Tell us a little about yourselves and why you want to work with us."

"Work!" I blurted out. "We feel God is calling us to be a part of this ministry. It's His call upon our lives that's brought us here today." We both took turns in telling our story of the call. They in turn asked several questions:

"How would you deal with certain behaviors in children?"

# The Encourager

"How well would you be able to cook for fourteen people?"

"Can you drive a van full of children?"

We answered every one of their questions and more until they said, "We will be in touch with you in the next couple of days. Thank you for coming."

"Yes, thank you," they all said in unison, and with that Alan escorted us out by another door. Checkbook in hand, he asked what our expenses were, as he prepared to write us a check.

"Even if we don't get the position, we don't want to be reimbursed," Jim told him. "Put the money in the children's home. If God wants us here, He will provide," I said.

We left and Alan's face was pure delight. He said in a most English accent, "Well, I never." His voice trailed off with a smile.

On the way to the bus station, Jim and I chatted about how the meeting went and what we should or shouldn't have said, but one thing stuck in my mind and that was what one of the committee members said to a question I answered.

"This is the kind of thing we're looking for," he'd said,

as he looked back and forth at the other members. I still couldn't get Linda and Ian off my mind, though. They were missionary kids. We were from Glasgow with no training. Nothing! Except, Jesus.

Two days later we got a letter in the mail. Postmarked London. I could hardly breathe. Opening the letter up it read, "We are pleased to welcome you to the Fegan's Family and at your earliest convenience let us know if you can join us at our yearly get together with all the other house parents at Pilgrim Hall."

My first reaction, to my own surprise, was a prayer.

*O Lord, what's going to happen to Linda and Ian? They will be so disappointed. They wanted this every bit as much as we did. Please give them Your peace.* That was my prayer. I felt so bad for them that we got accepted and they didn't.

I called Jim at work. "We got it!" I yelled over the phone.

"Got what?" Jim said.

"We are going to be house parents at a place called

## The Encourager

Little Dumpton in Broadstairs Kent!"

The next thing about floored me. Jim said, "Do you think we are doing the right thing?"

"Yes!" I shouted back. "God's calling us to serve Him."

"Just kidding!" He said. "I'll tell my boss right away. I'll give my notice now."

*Now we were on our way*, I thought.

Jim gave his notice. Mr. Haigie gave him a good farewell. Some of his mates thought he was crazy giving up a good job with a stable company to go to a place we had never seen or heard of.

Never mind the fact that we didn't know how much we would be paid, or what holidays or time off we would get. We didn't care. God had called us and that was sufficient for us.

## THE MOVE

*Pilgrim Hall Surprise*

The time arrived for us to leave. We said our goodbyes to our parents, relatives and friends, and contacted a moving company to move our stuff. I packed a few clothes for our family, as it would take about three days before we would reach our final destination.

We had a white rabbit called Snowy (of course). Snowy was in a box Jim had made for him, and was put in the back of our station wagon along with our suitcases. The three kids were in the back seat, Jim was in the driver's seat, and I was the navigator.

Jim and I left a key with my friend Ann, who was going to let the movers into our house when they arrived to pack up all our furniture and things. We completely trusted the Lord in all of this, never giving a thought as to what could happen if the movers didn't show up or if Ann forgot to come to the house.

## The Encourager

Everything in the house was just as it was when we lived in it. We simply left a note that said, "Stove and washing machine stay, but everything else, including carpets, are to come to Broadstairs, Kent." And then, we left!

God is so good! He really does take care of us. And He did. We had asked the telephone company to keep our phone connected for a couple of days after we were gone so that we could check on the movers to make sure they got everything right, and not pack stuff that belonged in the house, like the stove and washing machine.

The trip to England was good. We stopped overnight at a Bed and Breakfast, and the kids, as well as the rabbit, did very well. After a night's rest and a hearty breakfast of sausages, eggs and toast, we set off for Pilgrims Hall in Tunbridge Wells, Kent.

On the way, we checked in with the movers. Jim found a call box (no cell phones in those days) and we talked with one of the guys who was loading up the truck.

"Is the breakfast set to stay or go?" He asked.

"It's to go!" I said. "Only the washing machine and stove stays. Everything else comes down to Broadstairs!"

## Dot Goldie

Jim began to panic a little, and I have to admit, I did too. So, we thanked God that at least the man had answered the phone when it rang. *What if he hadn't?* He also told us that Ann had not showed up. To this day, we have no idea how the movers got into our house in Dalkeith.

Our family finally arrived at Pilgrim Hall, a beautiful old building and manicured gardens, very much like a palace. We were ushered to our bedroom, where we freshened up before going down to the main hall to meet the rest of the house parents, who had already arrived and were enjoying the splendid hospitality of Pilgrim Hall.

As we approached the dining room, we were greeted by no other than Linda and Ian Williamson. I was astonished to see them, of all people!

"What are you doing here?" I asked Linda.

"We have been here at the home in Canterbury for two weeks," she said. "We were chosen for that home. You and Jim got Little Dumpton. That became vacant the day of the interviews, so we both got hired!"

Initially, it was Canterbury that needed house parents. Then on the day of our interview the couple who were in

## The Encourager

Little Dumpton, as it was affectionately called, handed in their notice. How's that for a miracle?

"Linda, I prayed for you when we got the news that Fegan's picked us instead of you," I told her.

"And we did the same when we got our letter!" She said.

Neither of us knew that there were two vacancies. We thought we were applying for the same position.

*Oh, God, You are so Awesome!* It's all we could think about, as love rained on us at Pilgrim Hall. We had a new family now.

## NICK, NICK AND MARIE

We met Nick and Marie Wibmer, the house parents in the all boys home in Broadstairs, which was ten minutes away from Little Dumpton. The Wibmers had been doing this work for ten years.

The other Nick was our assistant, who made his journey to Pilgrim Hall alone. Ann, the other assistant, was at Little Dumpton packing. She was leaving the next day with the former house parents. So, we didn't know what to expect when we eventually arrived at Little Dumpton.

The night before, during dinner at Pilgrim Hall, Marie had informed us that we would spend the night at their home with the boys, as that would allow the other set of house parents to pack and leave before we moved in.

I thought, *Good, that's really sweet.*

"Nick will show you Little Dumpton first and then take you to Sunnyholm for the night."

## The Encourager

All was going well. Everyone loved us, and we love them in return. Then it was time to go "home."

It was a gorgeous sunny day. Everything was bright and at Pilgrim Hall. It was all wonderful. And then, we arrived at Little Dumpton.

## LITTLE DUMPTON

It was pitch dark. There were no outside lights, only the light of the moon and the stars lit up the sky. Nick opened the huge garden gate that scraped along the ground as he forced it open, and headed toward the kitchen's back door.

"We use this door most of the time," Nick said, a he opened the door. A wave of smelly, sweaty feet greeted us. I looked down and saw stacks of children shoe boxes.

*What in the world?* Was my immediate reaction, but I didn't say anything, simply looked around at the small kitchen area. We proceeded to the dim hallway, which led us into a huge dining room, with two large oval dining tables. They were set for breakfast, seating about ten people each. As we walked through the dining area and onto the main hallway of the home, we were met with the smell of urine coming from the upstairs toilet.

## The Encourager

Then we saw the children! They were in what was called their living room, watching some show on a black and white television. They were the meanest looking bunch of kids I had ever seen. Their hair looked greasy, their clothes had holes in the sleeves, and they were seating on furniture that was all torn up, with about 15 little pillows all over the place.

No one talked to us except Julie and Una.

"Hi,'" they said and then went back to watching the TV. I felt such oppression in that room. Something was not right. Nick introduced us to what would be "our" living room and to the outgoing house parents and assistant. We exchanged greetings and the house father said, "These are the RULES!" Pointing to a NO SMOKING IN THIS ESTABLISHMENT sign on the hallway wall.

*That's Going!* I thought, as I looked around the room. The fireplace was a mess; the cabinets on either side were smashed as though something had been thrown at them. The walls by the door had stains running down them as if tea had been splashed or thrown on to it. The carpet... Oh, the carpet! Where to begin? It was a horrible turquoise blue that had seen better days. There were boxes everywhere. I thought it must be their stuff, but NO! Nick said that it was always like this.

Then, I saw a cane on the wall.

"What's this?" I asked.

"That is for the kids if they misbehave," Nick said. I was horrified! Had I left my nice, clean, new house for this? I talked to God saying, "Surely Lord, for the first time in Your life, You made a big mistake!"

After taking our leave of the house parents, Nick took us over to Sunnyholm. We still could not see very much in the dark as we drove. Marie greeted us at the door and warmly invited us in. She ushered us into her living room that was warm and cozy and .

"Well, goodbye, I'll see you in the morning," Nick said and left.

In the meantime, Marie made us a welcome cup of tea and tea biscuits. All was quiet at sunny Sunnyholm; everyone was in bed, except for Nick and Marie.

Marie was a well-rounded, motherly figure, very English, while Nick was a former captain in the Gimkus in

# The Encourager

India. He was very tall and straight, stiff upper lip and all that. They had a son Marcus and a daughter Genna, who lived with them. Marie had a daughter from a previous marriage who was married and lived elsewhere.

"Let's show you to your room for the night," Marie said as she led us upstairs. Everything was shining and clean in this house and I wished I could stay here in "Sunnyland" instead of that "Little nightmare" of a place. When Marie opened the door there were our beds—five hospital beds that were very high off the floor, with red sleeping bags on each bed. The kids thought it was great. Big high beds. I got them settled while Marie That'sthe English way of saying she'd run a bath for me to soak in and relax. She could see I was drained from all the travel and day's happenings. To tell the truth, I was very discouraged with what I had seen at Little Dumpton.

"Darling, come, your bath will help you sleep," Marie said. I went into that old fashioned bath, tears brimming from my eyes. Still wearing my glasses, I slid into the warm soothing bubbles when my eye caught a plaque on the wall at the end of the bath. It was a Scripture verse that changed my whole outlook forever. It was from Isaiah 41:10: *"So do not fear, for I am with you; do not be dismayed, for I am your God. I will strengthen you and help you. I will uphold you with my righteous right hand."* It was as though God Himself spoke clearly to me in the quiet of that bath. I tell you, that was the most beautiful bath I have ever had, and in perfect timing to get me back on track. I got out of the bath and into my bed. I looked over to see the kids were fast asleep, and Jim was almost there too. We said our goodnights and prayed. Jim went out like a light, but I lay awake for ages just thinking of all I had given up. The tears just flowed as I lay in the darkness of the room. I don't know if what happened next was real or a dream, but I was asking God what I was going to do. All of a sudden, it seemed the ceiling opened up and I saw a beautiful deep blue sky filled with stars. I heard a voice that seemed to say, "I have given you a roof over your head, clothes to wear, food to eat and a job to do. Now get on with it. I am with you and have gone before you to prepare the way."

    I still don't know if I really saw or heard that, but I remember it as though it was yesterday. I do believe God spoke to me. I fell asleep and that was it!

# The Encourager

## OUT WITH THE OLD

*In With the New*

The next morning Sunnyholm was filled with life, with boys everywhere getting ready for school. Marie told us to wait in the living room and our breakfast would be sent in to us. Sure enough, eggs on toast, cereal and milk, all on trays, and a pot of tea arrived. It was so nice. I was so rested and ready for the day ahead, whatever it held.

*Was I up to the challenge?* I would know soon enough. We said goodbye to Nick and Marie and set off for our "new home". We passed The English Channel, gleaming in the brilliant sunshine, the most beautiful sight I had ever seen in a long time. Then we saw it.

This beautiful mansion sitting high upon a cliff top. What a place, what a sight! In the daylight everything was different. We sat in the car and prayed before we entered the front door. We asked God to go before us into every nook and cranny of that house that His Spirit would pervade every room in Jesus' name. We walked in and saw how the sun filled every corner of that big hall. Then we noticed the cleaning lady there, who looked at us. "This is my last day," she said, but this bold announcement didn't bother me one little bit.

God was in the house now and He was doing some cleaning of His own. The next people to leave where the old house parents. The kids had left that morning for school and would return to new parents.

*How would this all go?* I wondered.

In the meantime, I was becoming anxious. My furniture from Scotland hadn't arrived yet. While we waited, I pleaded with Jim to lift up that turquoise carpet out of our living room. I hated that carpet with a passion.

"I rather have concrete than that!" I told Jim, and so he set to work and got that thing out of there. I was so happy to see it gone, and no sooner he had finished doing that when the movers van pulled up outside the house.

Everything made it safely.

We set to work getting my carpet down and putting my furniture in place. *Now, this is "my" home*, I thought as I saw everything transforming.

## The Encourager

The children all came home from school and it was as if we had been there forever. Actually, we were the fifth set of house parents that had come to "Little Dumpton" in the ten years since it had opened.

No one stayed very long. All the children had been there since the beginning so they had seen many changes over the years. But we had come to stay and stay we did—for five years.

On that first day, we also met Rhoda Claringbold (a.k.a., Auntie C.), one of the most wonderful ladies I have ever come across. She was 74 years old and had worked at Little Dumpton for ten years, riding an old bicycle called the iron maiden, with a basket on the front, about twelve miles a day from Ramgate to Broadstairs.

Auntie C. was the staff cook and baked cakes for the kids three times a week. We became close friends during the five years we were there.

What a blessing she was to us all!

"You know, you're holding things well, I don't think you need me here anymore," she said to me one day. "I think I'm going to leave."

## Dot Goldie

"You are staying!" I said, and a big broad smile broke all over her old wrinkly face. She was beautiful, a wonderful cook and strong Christian, and so loved by all who knew her, especially the kids in the home, including my kids.

# The Encourager

## BIG CHANGE IN LITTLE DUMPTON

One of the first things we changed in the home was the clothes the children were wearing.

"Is there any money available to buy new clothes for the kids?" I asked the accountant.

"There's plenty of money!" He said, and that was all I needed to hear. I immediately called the family into the kitchen and told them, "We're going shopping!" New school uniforms were purchased and three sets of Sunday clothes each, and new shoes for everyone. The delight on the faces of those kids was incredible.

It was my impression that if they felt good and looked good, they would be good, and it worked! Then we started on the furniture in their living room. Everything but the curtains and the carpet went. We bought good, used furniture from ads in the paper. A nice three-piece suite, a gold color that matched the carpet and curtains. We also got a nice stereo unit in place of the old record player. Someone donated a

## Dot Goldie

piano to us, which made a nice addition to the living room. There was a big square dining table by the bay window with six chairs, which the kids did use to do their homework. We bought beds and new bedspreads for all the kids and painted the whole house from top to bottom.

The teachers at school asked us what we had done to cause such a change. We told them it was the love of Jesus.

One evening we had a big bonfire. At the top of our garden there was a pit, where we burned the weeds and rubbish from the garden. Jim piled all the old furniture there and set it alight! The neighbors were worried when they saw the fire and called the fire department. But all was under control and the fireman left us alone. The kids had a great time. We sang and danced around that fire, and told the story of Shadrac, Meshack, and Abednego.

The eyes of the little ones sparkled with amazement and wonder as to why they didn't get burned up. We stayed up late that night to make sure the fire was totally burned out, as we didn't want any sparks flying and setting the grass on fire. We all had fun until we couldn't stay up any longer.

# The Encourager

## THE FAMILY

There were many other changes in the family in the early days. Some of the kids that had been in care for ten years either became of age (17 years old), where they had to leave us. Fegan's Homes social worker found them jobs and places to live or in the case of the Llewelen twins, who went back to their parents.

The family consisted of Michael Davis, 17, his sister Pauline, 14, from London; Julie, 14, and Adrian Davis, 13, a black African brother and sister from London; Christine and Michael Llewelen, twin, 14-years old; the Johnsons: Una, 14, Sara, 8, and Tommy, 3, of Irish decent; Michael, 12, Clive, 10, Audrey, 8 and Rodney, 5 (he had cerebral palsy) from Kingston, Jamaica, but lived in London until they came into our care. Then there was Ruth, 7, and Natie, 6, two little Jewish kids abandoned by their parents. Their grandma brought them to us.

## Dot Goldie

There were also my own three kids, who made up the rest of the "family"— Derek, 11, Alan, 8, and Sharon, 2 and a half. That was our family!

Some behavior problems still existed for quite some time, but with some tough love and lots of patience, we made it through.

Mike Davis was a dark, longhaired demonic looking boy. He was evil and didn't care about anyone or anything except himself. At 17 years old, he still wet his bed up until we came. The former house parents washed his sheets and cleaned his bed up for him. He was defiant in every way imaginable, but he met his match in me.

"You have to wash your own sheets and clean yourself and your room up or you are out of here!" I told him one day.

I did all the ironing and washing of clothes for the family, but I honestly felt he deliberately wet the bed for attention.

"I don't need you or anyone else. I can manage on my own!" He replied.

"Okay then, I won't wash or iron your clothes. I won't make you breakfast, dinner or tea. I won't take you to school.

## The Encourager

You can walk." I said. He soon got the message. Every time he went to make something to eat I would say, "I bought that! You said you didn't need me!"

If he would want to wash something I'd say, "That's my soap." Then one time he needed his precious denim jacket ironed because he was going to the Cinderella Club, a youth center in town.

Finally, he gave in and said, "I need you; will you help me?"

I fell all over him and said, "That's why I'm here! To love and care for you as if you were the only person here!"

I took the jacket and pressed it until it was perfectly smooth. He took it from me and put it on and for the first time in a long while he said, "Thanks, Auntie Dot!" And went on his way. Mike left us soon after that and we never heard from him again.

His sister Pauline was also a piece of work. She had a temper and was a thief, just like her brother. She stole money from my bedroom. Previously, all the doors to the house parents' private quarters and the assistants had been locked, but I felt that it was like a jail, having to lock and unlock doors

## Dot Goldie

all day long. So I told them, "no more locks." This was our "home," not a prison, and we were family, not prisoners. We opened our living room for anyone to come in and sit and watch TV or talk or listen to our music.

Soon it was really like family, but Pauline broke the rules not only at home, but also outside. She stole someone's checkbook and was caught by the police, and put on probation.

"If this happens again, you're out the door," I told her. "I will help you in any way you need, but you will have to change your ways, and only Jesus can do that." She never did accept the Lord, as far as I know.

One day she attacked me for telling her to get ready for a doctor's appointment. She kicked, scratched and bit me, but I was able to take her down before Jim and Nick pulled her away. We had her removed from the home.

You win some and you lose some. But we never gave up, no matter how hard it became. We still loved on them.

# The Encourager

## ADRIAN

Adrian was a big, tall black handsome boy. But oh, what a terror! He would throw furniture at us whenever he was in trouble. He had A.D.D. and was forced to take medicine by the previous house parents. But I felt the Lord said, "No More!" So we took him off it. It was tough going for a while but eventually through much prayer and laying on of hands, deliverance came and Adrian was set free. Those whom Jesus sets free are free indeed!

Adrian and I had a few run-ins. Once he came at me with a knife.

"I'm going to cut you in little pieces," he said.

"I'll love you anyway," I said, as I caught his hand.

"Jesus is my protector and you can't do me any harm." Somehow the knife fell on the floor and I felt a power go through me as I held on to his thumb and brought him to the floor. I put my foot on his face and told him, "You can't win this fight. Jesus is on my side." Then, I let him get up. He went to his room and later apologized for his behavior.

One day he got into a fight with Nick, our assistant. Once again, the enemy took over his body. He was foaming at the mouth and both Nick and Jim had a hard time subduing him. I was going out to the hall where all this was going on and I immediately recognized the enemy at work.

"Satan, come out!" I commanded in a loud voice. I prayed the blood of Jesus over all of us in the household, and in Jesus' name that demon left. Adrian became limp all over and Nick carried him upstairs to his bedroom and laid him on his bed. He lay there motionless for a time, so we left him for a while to rest. He was totally washed out.

A little while later, I went up to his room and explained to him what had just taken place. I shared the Gospel with him and he accepted Jesus as his Savior. From that day on, Adrian was a changed young man. Later on, when he left us, he came back to visit and shared with all the kids what he used to be like. He was a handsome boy.

# The Encourager

## RODNEY

Rodney was one of four siblings handicapped through cerebral palsy. He had a brilliant mind but his body was a mess. He was only five years old when he came to us. His brothers Michael and Clive were twelve years and ten years old, respectively. His sister Audrey was eight years old. They were really a nice family, but I thought I'd never be able to look after Rodney. His needs were great and we had our hands full with the rest of the troubled kids; however, the social services in London did not want the family split up. So, we had to take him in.

    Rodney came in a wheelchair, as he couldn't walk, and he talked with a slur. He couldn't dress or clean himself, or hold a knife and fork to feed himself. Everything had to be done for him. I felt overwhelmed, but God reminded me that "He was my Helper and He would work with me." I was not alone. As it happened, there was another home nearby for handicapped children. Jean Hammond was the person in charge. She was a wonderful lady, who offered to take Rodney during the week and teach him some things that he could do for himself and then he would come to us at weekends.

    This was all cleared by the social workers involved, and so Rodney's lessons began. It was only a matter of two to three weeks before Rodney could put on his watch. That was the delight of his life—his watch. He also learned to put on his clothes. Jean was a miracle worker in my eyes! She taught him to use a knife and fork so he could sit at the big table with everyone else at dinner.

    In no time, Rodney moved back into Little Dumpton and became part of the family. He was given no special treatment and had to do everything for himself, including climbing upstairs to his bedroom. He was fitted with two walking sticks and had special steel toe capped boots specially made for him, and wore braces on both of his legs. He became very adept to running with all the paraphernalia on him. He never went back into that wheelchair, ever! On the contrary, Rodney went everywhere we did, and no one helped him. He had to keep up with the rest of us, and he

## The Encourager

did. Sometimes, though, he would put on an act in front of strangers and make believe he was tired or he would fall down deliberately to get attention.

One day, we were out for a walk. There were lots of older people walking along the promenade and Rodney fell. I turned around and looked at him.

"Get up, Rodney!" This old lady tried to help him to get up, but she couldn't. He was much too heavy for her.

"Please, leave him. He can manage by himself," I said, as I walked on.

"You are a cruel woman!" She yelled after me. "You should be reported."

I turned and said, "Rodney, let's go!"

He was up and going like the clappers, as we say in Scotland. He ran past that old lady before she could blink.

"You nearly got me into a lot of trouble, Rodney," I told him. "Don't put that act on again or you'll have to go back to Auntie Jean's."

Although Jean did a marvelous job with Rodney, he did not like being with the deaf, dumb and blind handicapped kids at Jean's place. He wanted to be with us. So one warning

## Dot Goldie

was enough. He never did that again. Rodney had many medical problems and was in and out of hospital a lot. He had pins put in his ankles, he had eye surgery on both eyes, and he had speech therapy and more. But the two things that stand out are the miracles done by the Lord.

When Rodney had his eyes done, the doctor told me, "He's going to have a lot of pain, but just give him some children's aspirin."

"OK," I said. We were to come back to see the doctor in one week. I took him home and put him to bed, and he got special treatment from everyone. I prayed with him and stayed with him until he fell asleep. Then I went to bed.

At 4 a.m. I got up as usual to have my quiet time with the Lord. It was at that time I heard Rodney whimpering. I was reading my Bible at the time and I asked the Lord what I could do for him. I had been reading about how Jesus healed the centurion's servant and raised the widow's son from his coffin in Luke's Gospel.

*Lord, tell me what to do for Rodney*, I prayed, and the answer came immediately.

He said, "Lay your hands on him and say, 'Be healed.'"

## The Encourager

So, I got up and went into his room and soothed his head with my hands.

"I just talked to Jesus and He told me to lay my hands on you and say, 'Be healed', is that OK with you Rod?"

"Yes," he whimpered back. So I obeyed the Lord's command and put my hand over his eyes and said, "Be healed." Nothing more, just, "Be healed."

Karen, our new assistant, had heard him crying also and had gone to the medicine cabinet to get some aspirin. She gave it to him with a sip of cold water, and then I tucked him in under the blankets and kissed him.

"Rod, I thank Jesus for healing you," I said. "Stay in bed when the others get up for breakfast and I'll bring you breakfast in bed. You can have the day off school."

I slipped out quietly as he laid his head down to sleep. I went back to my quiet time and finished my daily devotional. Then I got dressed and went down to prepare breakfast for everyone. To my utter amazement, Rodney was down first, fully dressed and ready to go to school.

"What are you doing up? You should be resting in bed!"

# Dot Goldie

"But Auntie Dot, Jesus healed me!"

I was standing over the stove making pancakes for breakfast when he said that. I nearly dropped the batter I was holding in my hand onto the floor. I laid everything down and went over to where he was sitting and looked at him intently.

"Do you have any pain anywhere in or around your eyes?"

"No," he interrupted. "Jesus healed me after you left my bed. Jesus healed me!" He exclaimed.

"You can still have the day off school…"

"No, I want to go to school!"

"No, Rod, you should stay home, at least for one day," I insisted. I called the doctor's at Thanet Medical Hospital and asked for an earlier appointment than next week. They obliged and set up a meeting with the surgeon who had operated on Rodney's eyes for double vision.

The day arrived and we drove to the hospital. The nurse checked him and took his vital signs and filled in his chart. Then in came the doctor. He was all business, looked into Rodney's eyes, looked at his chart, looked again at Rodney's eyes, and then looked up at the nurse.

## The Encourager

"Is this the same Rodney Greenland's chart that we operated on a few days ago?"

"Yes, doctor," she replied.

"Amazing!" Said the doctor. "There is absolutely no scar tissue anywhere to be seen. His eyes are perfectly normal!"

The doctor looked at me, and just then Rodney smiled that toothy smile of his and exclaimed, "Jesus healed me!"

I explained to the doctor what had taken place that morning at 4 a.m. He was absolutely stunned and wrote right in Rodney's record chart: *A miracle! This child had major surgery on both eyes and there is no sign of any scars. He is completely healed.*

So it is to this day on Rodney's chart: God healed him. Praise God!

That's not all that God did for Rodney. He also had several surgeries on both legs, and lots of physical therapy. We prayed for him daily for complete healing and that one-day he would walk unaided. We had a prayer group meet at Little Dumpton every Tuesday morning. Some local supporters

# Dot Goldie

came faithfully every week for five years. A lady named Mary was one of them. At one of the early meetings, Mary had a vision during our prayer time.

"I see a young black boy standing straight and walking around," she said. "I think it's Rodney!"

Well, I was excited because I knew God had something special for Rodney after the healing of his eyes. That morning when I prayed over him and said, "Be Healed," the Lord had instructed me to pray for him every night. So, I did! I never said anything to anyone, I just quietly prayed over him every night.

Slowly, but surely, Rodney got stronger and stronger with each surgery, until one day he no longer needed braces on his legs. Then, he only had one stick and eventually, no stick. At last, he was walking on his own and I had the privilege of taking him for his first pair of shoes. During these changes, Rodney was moved into the same school as the other kids. He made it on the soccer team as goalie. His report card was A+. "Genius" was the word one teacher used.

Rodney was ten years old when he left Little Dumpton to return to London to live with his dad and new mom. Mary's

## The Encourager

vision had become a reality five years later. Rodney walked out the door unaided, with that big toothy grin all over his shining face. Yes, Jesus healed Rodney and he told everyone!

## COMING TO AMERICA

To this day, I am still in awe of how God brought us to America. The Lord had been preparing us for a big move, as things were coming to an end for us at Little Dumpton. We didn't know what we would do or where we would go. But, several Scriptures leaped out at us, as if they were written in bold capital letters.

**Matthew 19:29**.

Then, the Lord gave us Genesis 12:1:

He gave us a multitude of other verses from Isaiah, Psalms, Proverbs, John, Revelation, Timothy and Philippians.

Our friends Peter and Margaret Waugh also had been called by God to work in the Bahamas. Peter was an engineer, Margaret a housewife. Their two children Jamie and Leila were about the same age as Derek and Alan. They moved to the Bahamas at the same time we went to Broadstairs. During their time in Nassau, from time to time they would fly over to Florida to take the kids to Disney World.

## The Encourager

It was during one of their visits to Florida that they came in contact with the Rev. George Callahan, a Presbyterian minister from Pompano Beach, who was in the process of starting a church called New Covenant at Sample Square. It was just a shop front but then moved to Crystal Lake Middle School. George was a charismatic preacher, who loved everything about Scotland, and trained for the ministry in Edinburgh. Peter and Margaret were both born and brought up in Edinburgh so they immediately "clicked."

It wasn't long before the Waughs found themselves becoming more and more involved with George's ministry. They would fly over for services now and then. When they couldn't go, they began to get tapes of George's messages each week. Then they began to send us tapes to hear this man preach. We loved it. To tell the truth, it was these taped messages that got us through a lot of difficult times. God used George's voice to teach us His Word and change our lives like never before.

As time passed, Peter and Margaret and the kids came to visit us at Little Dumpton. "You need a holiday," they said to us when they saw all the work we were doing.

## Dot Goldie

"Why don't you come and stay with us in the Bahamas?"

"We will take care of it," said Peter. They had money. We did not. We were on a very basic wage at Little Dumpton. Room and board was free; wages were on the bread line. No extra money for trips anywhere except where we could drive to and Fegan's Homes organized churches to take us in and let us sleep on floors in their church halls.

So when the Waughs offered us a trip of a lifetime, we began to put things in motion. It was as if the Lord opened up the doors. Children were fostered out, no problem. Parents came and wanted their kids for the summer. No problem. Mike Davis left us for good. No problem! Our own three kids were invited to stay with our friends, Todd and his wife and family. The assistants were left with only Ruth and Natie in the home, everyone else was gone. Our committee agreed that we could go, so we were ever so excited. We were going to the Bahamas, to Florida and Disney World, and to New Covenant Church, in Pompano Beach!

# The Encourager

## IN AMERICA

We flew from London to Miami. Peter had booked us in at a big fancy hotel on Collins Avenue, right on the beach. I will never forget the first time we walked out of Miami International Airport. The heat! Oh, my! I thought my breath was taken away. I had never experienced heat like it. Jim and I were overwhelmed by all the hustle and bustle of people and the language. At first we thought we had landed in Cuba! Everyone was speaking Spanish.

Jim and I looked at each other in bewilderment.

"What's going on?" I asked Jim, who was as confused as I was.

"What's with the foreign language? I thought we were in America," said Jim.

Suddenly, a man approached us and asked in broken English, "What hotel?" Jim gave him the address and loaded our suitcases in the bus. Traffic was everywhere. Taxis, busses, cars, vans, trucks… all clamoring for spaces outside the terminal. Soon we left all that behind and our bus finally arrived at the Duville. It was the biggest hotel I had ever stayed in. Jim and I were in awe. The huge entrance, the chandeliers, the plush carpet. Everything was huge.

*We were in America.*

Jim checked us in. Peter had done everything he'd said he would. Our room was ready. A bellboy took our bags and we followed him to the elevator. When we reached our room the bellboy opened the door to the biggest room I had ever seen in my life. I'd only seen things like this in Doris Day movies. To our surprise, the room had plaid carpets (tartan, in Scottish language) and tartan wallpaper. We laughed. Only Peter could arrange something like that.

We quickly changed into shorts and T-shirts. It was too hot for anything else. Jim laughed at me. I had always worn panty hose, and never dreamed of going with bare legs anywhere. So I duly kept my hose on under my shorts, but as soon as we were out in the sun, I promptly returned to our room and removed them.

It was too hot.

I will give you all a laugh now, if you are not already

## The Encourager

laughing at the last statement. Peter had told us, "You must go to McDonalds; it's a great place!"

We had never heard of it, so we set out to find a McDonalds. We ordered our food and sat down at a table to eat. And suddenly we realized, there were no knives and forks to eat with. We never ate anything without cutlery before. How naive we were! That evening we looked around the big shops that were IN the hotel.

*Shops in a hotel?* We couldn't believe it!

*We were in America.*

And soon to be in the Bahamas! Our day in Miami was quite an experience. Everything was BIG. The buildings, the cars, the shops, the people! The next morning we woke up to a brilliant sunny day, and it was only 7:30 a.m.

We went for breakfast to the Texas Cafe that was nearby the hotel, and would you believe it? Our waitress was from Glasgow, Scotland! She had been in Miami for several years and longed to go back to Scotland, but couldn't afford to. We felt so sorry for her. We shared with her and told her Jesus could help her, but she would have none of it. We planted a seed and left it at that. Only God can change

## Dot Goldie

hearts. After our breakfast of two eggs "over easy" (I've always wanted to say that!) on toast with coffee galore, we went back to our hotel to pick up our stuff and get ready for our flight to the Bahamas.

"Where to?" The taxi driver asked.

"Chalks Airport!" We said. Peter had booked us on a sea plane. We had never been on a sea-plane before.

We arrived at the little shack of a place. A few others were ahead of us. There was mass confusion going on. People were upset because there were no seats on the plane. Jim joined in the fray of asking questions. There was a mix-up with booking and they were overbooked.

"But we have tickets!" Everyone said. I sat down on a big pile of wooden boxes and prayed. Every now and then, Jim would anxiously look over at me to see if I was all right.

"I'm just praying," I'd said to assure him. Then he'd go back to the desk and talk more to the people.

After about three hours past, all of a sudden a man appeared and told us that everything had been sorted out

## The Encourager

and then we all got on board. *Thank You, Lord*, I silently said, and smiled when I sat at my window seat. There was a piece of tissue paper stuck in the window. I looked at Jim and laughingly said, "This is to keep the water out!"

    He laughed so hard, we both did. I think it was just a way of relieving all the tension of the past three hours. Soon we were off, skimming across the water and finally rising high in the air. I looked through the water, as it splashed the window, down to the beautiful blue ocean below. It was so clear and clean. I'd never seen water so clean except when it came from a faucet! It was a fascinating trip, especially the landing on water.

    "We made it," everyone said, as the plane rolled up to the docking place. We all clapped our hands and thanked the pilot as we disembarked. Peter was there waiting for us.

    "How was your ride?" he asked beaming all over. He knew we had never experienced anything like this ever. He greeted us with big hugs and ushered us into his car.

    "Margaret's got our dinner ready when we get home," he said. "Mince and tatties."

    "I'm ready for that," said Jim.

## Dot Goldie

"Me too," I piped up, holding on to my seat for dear life. Peter is an erratic driver at best of times, but this ride was hair-raising. Jitney buses were dodging in and out and bikes and scooters were in the mix. It was a circus.

We finally arrived outside a beautiful town house that the Waughs had rented. It was huge in comparison to anything we had ever rented in Scotland.

The smell of mince and tatties filled the air. Margaret was all suntanned and beautiful as usual. Her smile and welcome was so lovely. They were genuinely so pleased we had come.

Jim and I had a great time with them. They took us everywhere. They gave us their spare car to drive ourselves to the beach or wherever we wanted to go on the island. I felt like a movie star.

We had all missed each other, and so every night we sat up late and had Bible study like we used to when we all lived in Scotland. It was super!

It was there that God spoke to us from Genesis 12:1: *"Go from your country, your people and your father's household to the land I will show you."* We all felt God was

## The Encourager

telling us the same thing but we didn't know the things would work out. We prayed and just said, "Thy will be done, Lord. We are Yours."

There was one night I thought we would die laughing. We always laughed when we were with Peter and Margaret. We still do to this day! But on this occasion, we were listening to a Bahamian preacher on TV. It was the last program before the station closed down for the night. His last words were, "Have a nice DEATH!"

You had to be there to appreciate it. We all fell laughing; it was so funny.

The Waughs treated us like royalty the whole time we were there. They invited us to church, whered we met all their friends. We got an invite to go speak to the students at Nassau Christian School. And I was invited to speak at the Women's Group at church and share about our ministry at Fegans House. It was the first time I'd ever spoken in a church meeting. It was all so great. God was so good. We praised Him for all His goodness to us, giving Him all the glory.

We stayed with Peter and Margaret for three weeks. For our fourth week, they had arranged a trip to Disney

## Dot Goldie

World for us and to stay with some lawyer friend of theirs in Fort Lauderdale when we returned from Disney. They had also arranged for us to meet George Callahan on our last day before returning to Broadstairs. It was all like a dream. We could hardly believe all this was happening to us.

Disney was fabulous. We were wishing our kids could see what we were seeing and do what we were doing. "Oh, God," I cried. "You are so awesome!"

After our three-day stay at Disney, we set off for Fort Lauderdale. Peter had made all the arrangements and told us that the key would be under the doormat of the house, and we were to let ourselves in, as the couple would be at a sports event.

"The mat says PRAISE THE LORD on it," he told us.

At first, the taxi driver couldn't find the place. He said with all the canals it sometimes was difficult to find the right place. Peter had told us that this couple lived in a prefabricated house. So I'm telling the driver this to try and help him find his bearings.

"There's nothing like that here," he said. Then he said, "Here we are!"

## The Encourager

Jim and I looked out at the house before us and said, "There must be a mistake!"

"Oh no," said the cab driver. "This is it!"

"Go see if the doormat says 'Praise the Lord' on it," I told Jim, and he got out of the taxi, went over to the door and looked. "Yes!" he called back.

"Is the key under the mat?" I asked him, and sure enough the key was there. The cab driver dropped our bags off, Jim paid him and off he went. This place was like THE WHITE HOUSE!

*Peter and his sense of humor. Pre-fabricated house, indeed! Wait until we talk to him,* I thought. We opened up the double doors into this beautiful, white carpeted, mansion house. A beautiful big golden long-haired Labrador greeted us. At first we thought it was going to attack us, but he just about licked us to death. He was so happy to see us.

We were afraid to go anywhere in the house. No one was around. The whole place was immaculate. We sat in the kitchen and read the note on the table that said, "Welcome Goldies, make yourselves at home. Max won't bother you, he's just a big pet. See you soon."

## THE BORDENS

It was only about 10 to 15 minutes before the Borden family arrived home. They greeted us like long lost friends.

"Peter's told us all about you guys. It's great to meet you at last," they said. We were speechless. These people didn't know us from Adam, yet they threw open their home to us for as long as we wanted.

Wow! What a place! This definitely was a millionaires place. We had never been in anything like this in our lives. The Bordens were wonderful. They showed us around and took us to church on Sunday.

I thought, *I'm in New Covenant Church*. Actually, it was the Crystal Lake Middle School. The place was bursting with people. The music minister was preparing the choir to start the service. It was all like a dream. People shook our hands and welcomed us. We had never experienced "Church" like this before. Then George came on the scene. He was short, bald on top, a shiny tanned face with a smile as big as the

## The Encourager

Grand Canyon. He wore a beige suit and a blue shirt with his "dog collar."

He was not what I imagined him to be.

I'd only ever heard his voice on tape and so I pictured him tall, dark and a head of hair! He was not a disappointment though. I had loved this man's voice and his messages for months, everyday in Broadstairs sitting in our living room listening to his tapes and now here we were... in his church, albeit it was a school auditorium.

The service was amazing, and the singing and music was wonderful. The time flew by, all two and a half hours of it. As we were preparing to get out, the choir sang a song to the tune of "It's a Small World." I loved that ride at Disney. Finally we met George. He reminded me of a showman. He shook our hands and welcomed us with his best Scottish accent and said, "Glad you're here. Let's go eat!"

Bonnie Callahan was a small, very slim blonde. She was a picture of perfection. We all got into cars, and several others came with us. We arrived at a place called Sizzlers. George sat with us and chatted about Edinburgh and his love of Scotland. Dinner arrived and we all talked over a delicious

## Dot Goldie

meal about what God was doing at New Covenant and the vision George had for the place. It was all very grand and exciting.

"I would love to be a part of that!" I said.

"We would love families like yours to be a part of it," he replied. "Let's pray and see what God does with it."

We agreed that we would pray and seek God's will, not ours, to be done. All too soon our meeting was over and it was almost time to go to the airport and fly back home to England and all the kids at Little Dumpton—back to reality and life as we knew it. It certainly was a trip of a lifetime. Praise God!

We left Miami about 11 p.m. The flight was delayed two hours. Jim and I were both very tired so we closed our eyes for a while and rested. It had been a hectic day.

We bought presents for everyone at Playworld, said goodbye to everyone who had showed us Pompano, Fort Lauderdale and Coral Springs. Everyone was so nice to us; it was wonderful. Now it was time to come back to earth. Our flight number was called and we boarded the plane. Soon we were flying high. The lights of Miami disappeared and then

## The Encourager

the only thing we could see was the night sky. We sat back in our seats and shortly after take off the flight attendant brought snacks and soft drinks. We also had headsets to watch a movie but I was too tired and soon fell asleep.

It was a long flight, about ten hours or so. I awoke several times in the night; my neck was sore, my feet were swollen. I just felt cramped all night. We had breakfast before landing in London. When we got off the plane, we knew we were home. It was cold, damp and dirty, especially when we got to Victoria Train Station to catch the train to Broadstairs.

Everything looked so dismal and dirty in comparison with Florida, where everything was bright and clean. On the train journey from London to Broadstairs, we stood the whole way, as there were no seats. The train was packed. Our suitcases and bags were balanced between our legs. What an end to a dream vacation! This was LIFE.

At Broadstairs, our friend Todd met us and drove us to Little Dumpton. All the kids were back. They made a huge banner for us that hung from the first floor balcony.

It read: "Welcome Home, Mom and Dad. We missed you!" Yes, we were home and glad to be there. We had missed them too. We had a wonderful reunion with our three kids. Sharon seemed to have grown so much. Derek and Alan were very mature looking too. We never realized how much we really did miss them until that very moment.

All the other kids clamored around us and hugged us and told us how glad they were to be back and to have us home again. What a welcome indeed. It was great to be home at last!

# The Encourager

## CHRISTMAS IN AMERICA

It was the year after our first visit to America that we decided to take our kids with us to see what America was like. We had kept in touch with George and New Covenant and they invited us to come back. We made arrangements once more for the Fegan's Home family to be cared for and once again the Lord opened the door for us to go.

Our kids were excited to say the least. Going to America for them was a big thing. To tell the truth, I could hardly contain myself. I was as excited as anyone.

George made arrangements for our accommodation. A lady by the name of Chris Greenman was taking us into her home. Chris was a widow and lived in a beautiful home built by her late husband. It had a big swimming pool, four bedrooms, double garage, living room, dinning room, kitchen and family room. It was beautiful. Chris was a first grade teacher at a local school in Boca Raton. She had responded to George's call during a church service for someone to

## Dot Goldie

house this Scottish family for the Christmas holidays.

We arrived at Miami International Airport. This time we were prepared for the heat, language, traffic and people. We had no idea who Chris was or who was coming to pick us up. We got through customs and had picked up our luggage and went outside and waited on the sidewalk.

All of a sudden a dark haired woman walked up to me and said, "Hi. Are you the Goldies? I'm Marsha Wolfarth. Dave, my husband, is waiting over there."

She pointed to a huge yellow station wagon and Dave was standing with the rear door wide-open, motioning to us to come over.

"How did you know who we were?" We asked Marsha, as we gathered our bags.

"We just simply asked God to show us the family of five and the tiny little redhead with glasses!" Yes, that's me. All five feet of me. "Out of all these people you were the only ones we went to," she said as she lifted a bag into the trunk of the car.

"What a big car," the boys said.

"It seats 12 people," Dave replied.

## The Encourager

"How was your trip? Did you have any problems coming through customs and all that?" Dave asked.

"No problems," Jim replied. "We have all been praying for you all," Marsha said. "Everyone has been signing up to have you all over for dinner. You are all in for a treat!"

We could hardly believe it. *People we don't know are signing up to have us at their homes. The Goldies?* We felt like V.I.P.s.

We finally reached our destination and pulled up outside this big house.

"What a lovely home you have," I said.

"Oh, this is not ours," they explained. "You are staying here with Chris." We went inside and were met by a young woman.

"Hi," she said. "Bring your stuff in!"

"Enjoy the house, it's yours for a week," an older woman said. "You'll be on your own for awhile."

"Who are you?" I asked.

"I'm Chris; this is my home but I'm going out of town for a few days. So make yourselves at home," she said. "Do the children swim?" She asked.

## Dot Goldie

"Yes, they do," I replied.

"Well they will have a good time here. Enjoy it!" She showed us around the house. Told us the refrigerator was full. Lots of cold cuts, chips, cheese, soda, iced tea! Salads, eggs, steaks. You name it, it was all there.

"Lots of people wanted you, but I got you!" she smiled. "I know God is going to do something special with you guys. I have to leave now, but my daughter Holly will pop in and out to see if you need anything. Besides her, I'm sure others from church will be dropping by to say hello. So, long! Enjoy," she said and left us in this big house by ourselves.

The kids loved it and couldn't wait to change into their swimsuits and enjoy that beautiful inviting blue water.

Jim looked at me in disbelief.

"Can you believe this?" he said. "They all just bring us here. They don't know us and leave us in this gorgeous big house all on our own."

Amazing how people trusted us with all of their stuff. We were both stunned, actually. And in shock at the generosity of this widow, Chris Greenman. We unpacked our bags and put everything away. The kids splashed around in

## The Encourager

the pool. Eventually Jim and I joined them and soaked up all this luxury that was ours for two weeks! That night we slept well. At first light, the kids wanted to swim. I made breakfast and we ate out on the porch. The kids were already in their swimsuits and could hardly wait to jump in. They had a ball, and so did we. A swimming pool in the back yard, and all ours.

Holly came by and brought the kids snorkels and flippers. She demonstrated how to use them by jumping in the pool herself. Holly is a great person, beautiful brown eyes, brunette colored hair and very thin. She is the youngest of five children, and has had lots of illnesses, but keeps on going. We loved Holly; she was lots of fun.

People dropped in on us from time to time and came by on Wednesday night to take us to New Covenant, where we met up with George once more.

He gave us a list and said, "This is all the folks who want you over for dinner. You won't have to cook anything while you are here." Again, we could hardly believe what was happening. Thirteen people signed up to have us over for dinner. One afternoon we drove ourselves over to the Boca Mall. Did I forget to mention George gave us his little green

## Dot Goldie

Golf VW to drive around in while we were here? We used it to drive up to Disney World. God just blessed us so much. The kids thought they were in heaven!

The day we went to the mall, we met George there. He was doing some Christmas shopping. He greeted us with a loud, "How are you doing?" and proceeded to pull out his wallet and handed $200 to us.

"We can't take that!" I said.
"You better take it," he said in his typical fashion, and threw it on the ground.

"Buy yourselves a Christmas present," he said. I was a bit embarrassed as I picked the money up from the floor.

"But George," I said. "This is too much!"

"Take it," he said. "Buy yourself a new dress for Christmas and get something for Jim and the kids. See ya!" He said, as he left. Once again we were astounded by the kindness and generosity. What a place this is. What a God we have that He should care for us like this.

Christmastime in Florida was like a fairy tale for us. All the beautiful homes were decorated with lights outside and snowmen and reindeer and Santas. We never had anything

## The Encourager

like this in Scotland. All we usually did was have a small Christmas tree with lights and ornaments on it, a few bits of tinsel here and there and hang paper chains and balls or bells from the ceiling and walls, and that was it. But in Florida... it was show time!

Chris had brown paper bags half filled with sand, and a candle was placed on top of the sand in each bag. About two dozen or so and she placed them around her front lawn and pathway leading up to the house. On Christmas Eve around dusk, she began to light the candles. She and all the neighbors in the street came out at the same time and as darkness fell, the street was glowing with a wonderful sense of peace and joy.

Chris told us that this was the tradition in her street and it was called "Lighting the way for Jesus," making it a welcome sight for all who came by. It was a beautiful thing to see. Twinkling lights on the rooftops and candles glowing in the dark. It was a lovely tradition, one of which I continued having when we finally came to Florida to live.

What a Christmas that was. Our whole family was blessed in an over abundance of gifts from our new family.

# Dot Goldie

## CATHERINE MARSHALL

### The Writer

One of our many dinner engagements was at the home of Catherine Marshall. Catherine had invited us to dinner because her late husband, Peter Marshall, was a very famous Scottish preacher, and she wanted us to meet him on a long-playing record so that we could hear his Scottish accent.

"It's just like yours, Jim!" She said, and our three kids were fascinated by all the events of the evening. We met Catherine's mother, who also was very charming, as well as Catherine's husband, Leonard Le Soured, who was the editor of Guideposts. But the thing that impressed us all the most was Catherine had servants—two beautiful black women, dressed in uniforms of pale blue button down dresses and pure white bibbed aprons. They served us our whole meal. The kids just gloated. We had never been in a home with maids before. Len carved the turkey with an electric knife. We hadn't seen one of these before either. All this was "firsts"

## The Encourager

for us. After our delicious meal, Catherine ushered us into her plush living room with beautiful antique furniture and big over stuffed sofa and chairs. There was a big old-fashioned record player in the corner of the room. Catherine's mother came in and sat down on one of the overstuffed chairs. She was a beautiful white haired lady in her 90s, and the picture of health.

"You must get some of our delicious grapefruit from our trees in the garden and take them home with you," he said.

"I'd love to," I replied. "The oranges and grapefruit are so juicy and sweet here."

"It would be really something to tell folks I got grapefruit from Catherine Marshall's garden," I said with a chuckle in my voice.

In the meantime, Catherine was looking through a pile of sermons on record and paper that she wanted us to hear and read.

With great pride she said, "I think you will like this one. It's my favorite." She proceeded to place the record on the turntable and she moved the arm of the record player onto the record. The needle on the groove of the record made a scraping sound for a couple of seconds then this booming Scottish voice began preaching the Word of God.

"Let us read from the Gospel of John," Peter's voice was commanding, to say the least. It was a wonderful experience to listen to such a famous preacher from Scotland who had a movie made of his life. Maybe some of you who read this will remember it. It was called, "A Man Named Peter."

That was one of the most memorable evenings I have ever spent in my whole life. Yes, we got a huge big bag of grapefruits to take home that night along with memories I'll never forget.

Catherine had also offered us her help to get our immigration papers should we decide that that was what God wanted for our lives. That night we got a phone call from another friend, Dr. Joe Lunsford. He knew we were at Catherine's and called to say his lawyer offered his services to get us our immigration.

George had been talking to people about us and how we had said how great it would be to be a part of New

## The Encourager

Covenant Church. He talked to different people and so the wheels were being set in motion. This was so unreal. Who were we that so many people wanted to help us get to America?

Leonard and Catherine were wonderful hosts that evening. Never in a million years did we ever think we would be in the home of a famous person such as Catherine Marshall. We all had a marvelous time, and I felt like it was all a dream.

On our way home that night we were very excited at the thought of all these people wanting to help us. Was God actually going to bring us to the U.S.A. and be a part of what He was doing in the Church called New Covenant? How ever could such a wonderful thing as that come to pass?

## FOLLOWING GOD'S PLAN

Dr. Joe Lunsford is an orthodontist in Boca Raton and Coral Springs, Florida. He had two lovely little girls whom he and his wife, Kenny had adopted. They were the same age as Sharon. Joe loved Sharon and wanted to fix her teeth, as they were a bit squint and spaced out. He said he would fix them for her, if we came to stay. He also said that he would do the same for the boys.

Joe got us an interview with his lawyer Charlie. He was not an immigration lawyer but he would do what he could for us. This all took place the day we were to fly home to England. It was amazing the difference a day makes. Here we were coming to Florida for Christmas with our wee family, and end up having a lawyer trying to get us immigration status. We told Charlie right up front, "We don't have any money for lawyer's fees!"

"Don't worry about it," he said. "It's taken care of!"

So Jim and I went on our way, not worrying, and

## The Encourager

Charlie started working on our behalf.

"It would be a lot easier if you stayed stateside," he advised.

"Yes, but we have to take care of things at the Children's Home, so we will have to communicate with you from there," Jim said.

We arrived home to a wonderful welcome. Everyone was happy we were back, especially the assistants.

"At last you're back!" Tim and Maria exclaimed with bright smiles. They were fantastic young people who had come to work with us. We all got along so well with each other and that was a huge blessing for us all. Sometimes it was difficult when an assistant would be a bigger problem than the kids in care. But these two were perfect.

Maria was of Italian decent and Tim was a proper Englishman or boy, I should say. They loved the kids and took great care of them, playing games and taking them out. They were both good cooks too. Maria's specialty was pancakes, while Tim's was toasted cheese sandwiches. Maria taught Alan and me how to play the guitar. A couple of the kids in care also picked it up. So we had a little band. I played the piano, so did Clive, Michael, Alan and Maria played guitar. In the evening when everyone was done with homework and chores we would have a jammin' session. Some of the girls were good singers too. So we had a lot of fun during those times.

Meanwhile, we kept in touch with Charlie but not much was happening. It was a very slow process. The U.S. Embassy was not very helpful. We could not get anyone to answer the phone calls we made and it took ten weeks for them to reply to our letter requesting forms for immigration. When we eventually got our forms, we filled them out and mailed them off. Again, we waited, waited and waited. It was a very discouraging time. Communication was practically nil. One of our house committee members told us that we didn't have a chance of getting in. Her sister had tried and was rejected and she had a good job to go to.

That kind of news was not very uplifting, , I kept telling myself, as well as telling others.

*How would He do it? How would the doors open for us to get to Florida?* I wondered.

# The Encourager

## THE PHONE CALL

One evening it was as if all Hell had let loose in the home. Kids were in trouble; another assistant had come and was causing all kinds of problems. I was upstairs in my room laying on the floor praying, Jim was working on a project for the house and had gone out to the garage.

Then it happened.

The phone rang.

I ran downstairs to answer it.

It was George Callahan.

"I'm in an elders' meeting at the church and one of the elders just offered Jim a job, if he wants to come work for him," he said. The elder was none other than Dave Wolfarth. He had a woodworking business and needed a skilled carpenter.

"Would Jim be interested?" Before he said anything else I burst into tears. I related to George all that had just taken place at the home and how I'd just prayed.

## Dot Goldie

"Then the phone rang and you offer Jim a job!" I cried, and then called for Jim to come to the phone. George got Dave on the other end of the line to personally ask him to come work for him. Jim was ecstatic, and so was I. All the former moments were in the past. Tears of sadness were now jubilant tears of joy.

We had a job offer, now all we had to do was get Charlie on it and get the paper work done, right?

Wrong. This was just the beginning of a long paper trail that led us up and down the proverbial Garden Path.

We made transatlantic calls back and forth for months and nothing moved. Then Charlie wrote to us.

"It would be a whole lot easier if you would come over and take care of things from here," he wrote, but that was not an option for us.

Several months later, after that initial phone call, Dave sold his company. The new owner still wanted Jim to come work for him. So papers were filled out again with the new job offer and new employer.

Once again the wait was on. Then came the bombshell. Tom, the new owner had a bad accident. He cut

# The Encourager

off two fingers while on the job and had to close down the business, as he had no one to carry on the work and couldn't afford to keep things running. It was all a big mess.

In the meantime, things in the home had settled again and everything was running smoothly. Then, I had a nervous breakdown. What with all the ups and downs, the highs and the lows, the excitement and then the disappointment—it all took its toll on me and I got very sick. I went to live in our little flat called The Upper Room, above our garage. Jim had converted the old coach house into a little flat for us to go to on our time off, and be with our own little family for a couple of days a week.

It was while I was recuperating in that little flat that we got yet another phone call. Our assistant came up to the flat and rang the doorbell and was calling out to Jim to come down to the house.

"You have a phone call from America!"

Jim and I had just been discussing what our next move might be. He had a newspaper with jobs that were being advertised to go to South Africa, and make a fresh start. Carpenters were needed everywhere. We had just finished

## Dot Goldie

reading all the positions available, when all of a sudden, Jim crushed the paper into a ball and said, "Has God not called us to go to Florida? Then what the Dickens am I looking at South Africa for?" And then the doorbell rang.

He ran downstairs and all the way down our garden lawn and into the house. It was our old friend Peter Waugh. He was now living and working in Florida. Margaret was back in Scotland preparing to sell their home and move out to Florida, and set up home there.

Peter told Jim he was in the office of a man named Dick Kimble, who was looking for a finish carpenter.

"I told him that I knew of one," Peter said, "but he is in England!"

Dick said, "Can you get him here? Call him now."

"So how about it, Jimbo?" Peter said. "Do you want the job? It's a three million dollar project. Renovating the pent house of Carnival Cruise lines owner, Mr. Ted Arison."

"Yes! When does he want me to come?" Jim said.

"Tomorrow if you can!" Peter said jokingly.

"I'll get on it right away, Peter. I'll get a ticket tomorrow morning and I'll be in the first flight out, OK?"

## The Encourager

"OK, Jimbo," said Peter. "We will be in touch. Let me know your flight plans and I'll meet you at the airport. Bye Jim!"

"Bye Peter, I'll call you soon."

Jim was all aglow and excited when he came back up to the apartment and related to me the whole phone conversation word for word. I was so elated myself. This news was medicine to my soul. Here we were, one minute looking through the paper for a job in South Africa, and then we get a phone call from Miami asking Jim to come A.S.A.P. Only God can do stuff like this.

I soon recovered from all that ailed me after the phone call. We made arrangements with Fegan's Home. Told them what was going on and Jim prepared to get his flight to Florida. I packed his suitcase, and as far as we were concerned if things did not work out for him with this job, then it would just be an added vacation for him. But I was sure this was it. I duly got all of Jim's clothes in that suitcase, because I believed he was going, and going to stay.

It was only a matter of two days, before Jim was ready to fly away. He said goodbye to Alan at the house, Sharon was staying with a friend so we drove over to the house so he could say goodbye to her. They both cried.

Derek and I drove Jim up to London to Heathrow Airport. It was a terrible tearful time. We had never been apart before. Finally, his flight was called and we kissed and hugged and held each other for as long as we could until finally he had to go. Derek and I watched him until he was out of sight. We had all prayed before Jim left; now it was all in God's hands.

It was a terrible ride home to Broadstairs. I cried all the way. Dear Derek was the man now and I'll never forget the comfort he was to me on that long journey back to Broadstairs.

He was my navigator. I had no clue where I was going. But he did, and got us safely home that day. Sharon, Derek and Alan all took it in their stride. They were confident everything would work out this time.

When Jim arrived in Miami, Peter was there to pick him up. They were both going to be living in his friend Bob's home in Boca Raton. Bob was a pilot and his wife Debbie was a stewardess. They had offered to put Jim and Peter up at

## The Encourager

their house until both men got their families back together.

The next day, after Jim's arrival, Bob drove Jim down to Miami to meet Dick Kimble at the Arison Penthouse on Collins Avenue. Dick immediately offered Jim the job.

"Can you start tomorrow?" asked Dick.

"Yes!" Jim replied.

"See you at 7:30 a.m.," Dick said.

"Tomorrow 7:30 a.m., I'll be here," Jim replied. It was only after he met Bob outside that it dawned on him.

"How am I going to get here? I've no car, no money to buy a car! No tools with me. How am I going to do the job?"

Panic. "Don't worry, Jim!" Bob said. "You can have this car. I don't need it. Debbie and I can use our other car to get back and forth to the airport. It will work out. Dick will have tools you can use until you get your own. God will work it out. You wait and see!" And so, He did! Everything worked out and Jim started work the next day at 7:30 a.m. sharp.

## Dot Goldie

## PASSPORTS

All was working out fine for Jim. Dick Kimble loved his work and had said to Jim, "I wish I had had you three years ago!" Jim was just glad he was there now.

Jim would call me in England and fill me in on all that was taking place. How church was and how everyone had taken him into their hearts and home, everything was going well. But he missed us all so very much. He said that only half of him was there, the other half was in England. He missed us so much.

Four weeks later Jim called.

"Sell everything and come on over!" He said excitedly. "You have to come, everything is good with the job. I'm earning enough now to get us a place to rent. Chris said that she would take us all back to her house until we find a place. Her daughter Deb is a part time real estate agent and she'll find us something." I hardly had time to speak.

"I've got a car of my own now too!" he said. "One of

## The Encourager

the ladies at church came up to me on Wednesday night and said to me, "God told me to give you my car for as long as you need it. God spoke to her about "me," he said excitedly.

"So Praise God for Pam Newman and her new job. I am now driving a brand new Toyota with 900 miles on the clock!" I'd never heard Jim so excited before. He was almost as excited as me now, trying to get everything said in one breath. Then I hit him with the bad news. I was in tears.

"What's wrong?" he asked.

"Have you not heard in America yet?" I explained. The passport office was on strike in Scotland. It had been on T.V. every night on the news. People were lined up outside the Peterhead Passport Offices. No one could get a passport. No one as answering the phones. All you got was a busy signal when you called. Jim was silent on the other end.

"Can't you come home and get us?" We only had one passport—a family passport, and Jim had it in America.

"No, I can't come," he said. "Apart from that, we don't have the money to fly back and forth."

"So, what will I do?" I cried.

"We'll pray," Jim said. "God will work on our behalf. Go

ahead, get rid of everything. We will trust the Lord to open doors for us."

"OK!" I replied, the tears streaming down my face.

I told Jim that I'd had a few Scripture verses about "giving" things away.

"Do whatever God leads you to do," he said. "Don't worry, things will work out. I have to go now honey, God bless. Love to the kids. I'll call you tomorrow," he said then hung up the phone. I remember that call as if it were yesterday. I sat on the floor and just cried. I had no idea how I was going to get a passport for both Derek and myself.

Derek was now sixteen and could no longer be in a family passport. He needed one of his own. I prayed myself to sleep that night.

# The Encourager

## TRAVEL AGENTS

I had bought tickets earlier for us to arrive in Florida for our 17th wedding anniversary. But I'd never anticipated a passport strike. I thought all I had to do was send away for them and they would be here on time for us to leave in July.

I had a brain wave that morning after Jim's call the night before. *I'll pop down to the travel agents office and ask them if they have any "news" on the passport situation* I thought.

I have never had to do things like this before. Jim always took care of travel arrangements and stuff like that. I didn't know what else to do. So I drove into Broadstairs Main Street to the travel agents. The girl behind the counter was very bright and cheerful. She was a lovely blonde haired shiny, faced girl. Very smart in her royal blue skirt, white blouse and hair up in a ponytail, tied with a big white bow.

*She was radiant*, I thought to myself.

"Can I help you?" she asked.

## Dot Goldie

"Yes," I replied. "I was wondering if you could tell me if there has been any news on the passport situation?"

"As a matter of fact," she said as she motioned to the big filing cabinet behind her. "We got something in about that," she said, as she slid open a huge drawer, and pulled out a green and pink sheet of paper and began to read to me. "You can go to the Post Office and get a Continental Passport. That will enable you to get to America!"

"Great," I said. "Thank you so much."

"You're welcome," she said with a big, bright smile. "Glad to be of service! Enjoy your trip," she said as I walked out the door. My heart was leaping for joy. I went straight up the High Street to the little Post Office. Money in hand, I approached the teller.

"I'd like two Continental Passports please," I said.

"Where are you traveling to?" He asked.

"Florida," I said with a big happy smile.

"I'm sorry, Missus. You can't go to America on a Continental Passport."

"But the lady in the travel agents office said I could," I said, feeling in a bit of a panic.

## The Encourager

"Look Missus, I work here and I would know if you could use this to go to America or not! I won't take your money for something you can't use. Next please!" he said, as he motioned me out of the way for the next customer.

I went outside, tears running down my cheeks. *What now Lord?* I cried. As I was walking back to my car, it was as though I heard a voice speak so clearly to me.

"Go to the Ramsgate Post Office!" That was all I heard. I got in the car and drove down into Ramsgate and headed to the Post Office. There were several people in there. The Ramsgate Post Office was a big spacious building, as it was the main post office for our area.

Two nuns and a priest were in line in front of me. As they went forward to the teller, I overheard them ask for Continental Passports as they were traveling to Lourdes in France. They got their passports and moved to one side of the counter. Then the teller called me up.

"I need two of these also," I said pointing to the nuns and priest as they put the passports away. She duly pulled out two beige colored cards and asked for names and address. I gave her the information.

# Dot Goldie

"That will be £10.00 pounds please!" she said. I handed her two five-pound notes and said, "Thank you very much," and walked away. I couldn't believe it!

*That was so easy* I thought.

I drove home to Little Dumpton. Derek was there.

"I got them!" I said, holding the passports high in the air.

"Good, mum," he said. "Now we can go."

"Yes, yes, we're going to America," I sang.

"What do we do now, mum?" Derek asked.

"We get our passport photos. Down at the beach there's a machine that takes black and white passport photos."

"Let's go," I said, and off we went. We sat inside the booth and we each got three or four pictures each.

"That will do," I said as the pictures slipped out the bottom of the machine where you put in the money. "Very nice!" We laughed. All we need is a number underneath, as they looked like mug shots. We didn't care. We had our passports, and our photos.

We were all set.

## The Encourager

When all the excitement died down, I had a look at the passports. Our friend Dan Binns had popped in to see how we were doing. Dan was a Lay Preacher at St. Lukes. He was 74 years old, and a great man of faith. He stood about 6 ft. 2 ins. tall, very slim and white haired. Always had a smile.

"Oh, no!" I exclaimed.

"What is it my dear?" He always called me that.

"Dan, it does say you can't go to America on this passport!" I cried.

"Now, now, my dear," he said in a comforting tone. "The Lord Jesus has a plan for you and nothing is going to stop Him from getting you to Florida to be with your dear husband. Let's pray."

Dan prayed a prayer of faith that lifted, not only me, but also Auntie C., Derek, and the rest of the kids that were in the kitchen at that time. "You wait and see," Dan said when he finished praying. "God has opened a door for you! It will all work out in His time!"

We sat and chatted over a cup of tea for a while, until he was sure I was all right.

"I'm fine Dan," I said.

# Dot Goldie

"Don't worry," he said. When Dan left that afternoon I ran upstairs to my bedroom. I laid down prostrate on the floor and cried out to the Lord. I don't remember how long I was there, but it was a long time. I read my Bible and my devotional and got comfort from God's Word.

The next day, I decided to go back to the travel agents just to make sure that what the girl told me was right. I went in and two young men were behind the counter.

"Can I help you?" One of them asked.

"Yes, I just wanted to double check with you that I can travel with a Continental Passport?"

"I don't know," he said, looking over at the other assistant sitting at a typewriter. "Do you know anything about that, Pete?"

"No, I don't," he replied.

"I was in here yesterday, and the girl that was here pulled papers out of that file cabinet and read to me, saying I could go to the U.S.A. on a Continental Passport!"

They looked at each other and said, "What girl?"

"The blonde!" I said.

"We don't have a girl that works here," they said. "Are

## The Encourager

you sure you have the right agency?"

"Yes!" I said. "You're the only one in Broadstairs! I bought my tickets here a few weeks ago. You served me, if I'm not mistaken."

"Well, Mrs. Goldie, we don't have a girl that works here!" I was so embarrassed I walked out.

*They must think that I'm nuts*, I thought as I stood outside.

Then, that quiet inner voice spoke to me so clearly,

*"Did I not tell you Angels will go before you?"*

## ANGELS

*Did God really send an angel to help me?* I wondered as I traveled home. Jim called me that evening and I told him everything. He was in awe!

"That's fantastic!" he said. "Now all you have to do is go to the U.S. Embassy up in London and get your Visas. Do you think you can manage that?" he asked.

"Yes," I replied. "Harris is coming to Broadstairs to stay for a week to say our farewells. Mavis and Shirley are also coming." Harris is my big brother and Mavis is his wife, and Shirley is their daughter. Shirley is one year older than Derek.

"Harris said he would take me to London to the Embassy," I told Jim.

"Good, then everything is set?" he said.

"I hope so," I replied.

"Alright then. I'll call in a couple of days and find out how it's going. Ok?"

"All right, I'll talk to you soon. Love you!"

## The Encourager

"Love you, too!" I said.

My brother and I had a good relationship. We worked together in our butcher shop for years. We both loved horses and worked with our own horses, Trotters and Pacers. Harness racing was our passion. When I was younger, I helped train and even raced them. I loved it. My brother is a Horse Whisperer, as far as I'm concerned. There is nothing he doesn't know about horses.

He, his wife and daughter came to visit us at Little Dumpton. We had a wonderful time together. My nephew Harris didn't come, because he was working with the horses and had to run the shop. He was getting married soon too.

Mavis had helped me pack stuff into boxes that I was going to sell. She picked out a few ornaments that she liked and I gave them to her. They were all my wedding gifts. But I felt God had said sell what you have and give to the poor and needy. So, that's what I did.

She picked out some things and I sold the rest. A dealer came and gave me £50.00 pounds for the box. Not much, but I got rid of it. I gave all my furniture away to my pastor and a young couple that was getting married. They

## Dot Goldie

couldn't believe I was giving it to them. It was all very nice stuff, but I didn't care. Harris and family took Derek and I up to London to the U.S. Embassy. When we arrived the place was crawling with people.

"You'll be here all day Dot!" Harris remarked.

"No, I won't," I said.

"Look at all these people," Harris said.

"Well, in my quiet time this morning the Lord said, *'Walk right up to the door and it will swing open.'* So I'm going right up to that door," I said pointing to the glass double doors at the entrance to the embassy.

"This I will have to see!" said Harris. My brother was not a Christian, so he did not know God's power to do the impossible. I did.

I walked straight up to the door. A Marine, over 6 ft. tall was standing guard, with rifle in hand. He looked down at me and said, "Can I help you Ma'am?"

I held out our documents and said, "I want to go to America!"

"Give that to me," he said. "Come back at noon."

I handed him all that I possessed and walked away. My

## The Encourager

brother stood with his mouth hanging open and said, "I saw that, and I still don't believe it!"

"Believe it!" I said. "We have to come back at noon."

In the meantime, we found a McDonalds just around the corner from the Embassy and had some breakfast. We all talked about what just took place and were in disbelief. I could hardly believe it myself.

*What did I just do?* I asked myself. Mavis and Shirley wanted to do some sight seeing, but I was too nervous and anxious to do anything.

"You go," I told them. Derek and I will go back and wait at the Embassy steps until noon. I can't do anything else," I said.

"I'll see you at noon," said Harris and they walked off to see the Palace. As Derek and I walked down Bond Street, we passed a store that had a big sale going on. the sign read.

I saw this huge gigantic suitcase outside at the doorway of the store. "Derek, we could get all our stuff in that case. What do you think?"

"It's awful big, mom," he said.

"But we could get most of our stuff in that one big

one and it would be less luggage for us to maneuver at the airport," I urged. "Let's buy it!" So, we went inside and purchased the suitcase. Ten shillings! What a deal. I'm five ft. tall. The suitcase was almost as big as me. It had wheels on it, so Derek and I strolled back to the Embassy pulling this giant of a suitcase along behind us.

Everyone on the street would look and smile at us as we hurtled along the bumpy pavement of Bond Street. But I didn't care. *What a bargain!* When we arrived back at the Embassy the crowd outside was unbelievable. Something strange was happening. No one was being allowed inside the Embassy.

"What's going on?" I asked a woman standing next to me.

"We have to line up under our letter of the alphabet," she said. Signs were hanging above the entrance to the Embassy A-D, E-H, and so on.

"Whatever letter your last name begins with you stand under that sign," she said. The last time I'd been at the Embassy I went in and sat around for hours. But this was most unusual. I made conversation with this woman until noon,

## The Encourager

when the doors of the Embassy swung open. The agents inside brought tables outside, and had the people stand in their appropriate lines and proceeded to give instructions. Seconds later other agents from inside the Embassy appeared on the scene, carrying boxes full of passports.

I stood in my line with Derek holding my hand. We prayed under our breath, "Please don't let them see that bit on the passport that says, 'Not for the United States of America.'"

*Blind their eyes to that, Lord,* I silently prayed. Then out of the blue, a big commotion began. A man at the front of the line began shouting and cursing at the agent. He had been refused a visa! My heart started pumping hard in my chest. I could physically see my chest racing in and out.

Derek gripped my hand. "We'll be fine, mom. Don't worry," he said.

After that the line began to move again. Then, another person was refused a visa, and he was shouting. "How am I going to get to America? I've got a funeral to go to!" He too cursed and swore, but all to no avail. He was refused and that was that. My heart was about leaping out of my throat by now. Two people refused visas and they had real passports, the black ones. Ours were beige cards that folded into three pages.

*How was I going to get through this?* I was panic-stricken. Finally Derek and I were at the front of our line. When the people in front of us received their visas the agent motioned us to come forward.

"Names?" she asked.

I choked a bit then said, "Goldie. Derek and Dorothy." She fingered her way through the box of passports in front of her. I was anxiously looking too. I only could see black passports, no beige cards. All of a sudden, she pulled out these two Continental Passports and handed them to me and said, "Have a nice trip!"

I took them from her hand and a rush of excitement and relief rushed through my body. I jumped up and down like a three year old and yelled at the top of my voice, "We are going to America!"

Derek looked at me in horror and said, "Mother, behave yourself!"

But I couldn't contain my joy. Some bystanders looked

on and smiled and said, "Good for you! Are you going inside that suitcase?"

We all laughed. Relief beyond belief was mine.

We met my brother, who was totally blown away by our story. "If I had not seen this with my own eyes, I would have never believed it!" We were all overjoyed. Everything God said He would do, He did.

*He is so Awesome!* Everyone was happy on the drive back to Broadstairs. I can't begin to express how I felt. I was relieved, yes, but drained at the same time. Happy beyond words, but thinking, *What's our life going to be like from here on in?* The still small voice inside me just calmed all my anxiety and fears. Over and over these words from Psalm 46:10 filled my mind: *"Peace, be still and know that I am God. I am with you."*

I tell you, it was a very special day in my life. I was so tired at the end of it that I fell sound asleep that night before I'd finished thanking God for all His blessings that day.

*Was that tall marine another angel?* I wondered as I fell asleep. Harris and his family left a couple of days later. And that's when I got down to the real job of packing that suitcase. It looked bigger now that I had it at the bottom of my bed. *What was I thinking? This has to be the biggest suitcase in the universe!* I laughed out loud. Then it suddenly dawned on me—maybe it's too big.

Too big to go on the plane.

Too heavy, as well.

I decided to call the airlines and they gave me specific weight and sizes. Anything more we would have to pay extra. I thought, *that's fine, I can take it and just pay whatever the extra cost would be.* My mind was at rest now.

The time was fast approaching for us to leave. All business was settled with Fegans House. All the children were either gone to live with parents or were adopted or fostered. Only Ruth and Natie remained. Auntie C. was gone too, as she had finally retired. Our young assistants were preparing to leave also, but they would stay until the new house parents arrived in August to take charge of the Day Care Center. Ruth and Natie were allowed to stay on at the home until they reached 17, then Fegans would find them work and a place to live. I delivered my three-piece suite to our pastor's home. Dave Richardson was a marvelous man

## The Encourager

who fearlessly preached the Word faithfully week after week. *Man, oh Man! Did I have a time getting him to receive a gift.* I knew he loved sitting on my Saddle Set, as it was called. Jim and I had had it specially made. Lovely soft chocolate brown leather, trampoline sprung bases on the chairs and couch. We had a ladies chair and a Gents chair.

David loved that big Gents chair. It had a high back on it and so a tall person could lean back and rest his head on the soft cushion. The ladies chair was the same only a bit shorter. Eventually, after much debate, he gracefully accepted it. He wanted to pay for it but I refused saying, "Do you want me to disobey what God has told me to do?" We both laughed as we unloaded the furniture from our van into the Manse that was their home.

The couple I gave my bedroom and dinning room furniture to asked me if I could keep it at Little Dumpton until their wedding, August 1st.

"Yes," I said, because I'd have a bed to sleep in until it was time for us to leave. Fegans agreed it could stay until August 1st too, so that was set. I had one piece of furniture left that I didn't sell so I thought the home could have it. But in the back of my mind I remembered God had said it would all go. So, I waited before saying anything to Fegan's Home about it.

Martin Granger was getting my Avenger Station Wagon. So all that was left was one piece of a wall unit that Jim had built. It was white formica. He had made it in two pieces and a lady I knew liked it, but only had space for one piece so I put it out in the hallway, so if anyone came in and saw it, they might want it.

So came the day we were to leave. Nick and Marie Wibmer offered to drive us up to London's Heathrow Airport and they saw the wall unit and offered to buy it, but I gave it to them. So all my stuff went as God had said.

Nick, our assistant, drove my car as we had arranged to meet Martin Granger at the Motor-way Service Station on the way to the airport. I was then able to hand over the car plus all the papers and give him the title to the car. It worked out beautifully.

We met him, handed everything over to him, and said our goodbyes and he drove off in his newly acquired car. His friend who had brought him couldn't believe I had just given

## The Encourager

my car away. Nick got in the van with the rest of us and we headed out to the airport. Both Nicks were a great help with that huge suitcase and the several other bags and cases we had—seven pieces altogether.

We got to the counter to check in, and the girl looked at us.

"Is this all yours?" She asked.

"Yes," I replied.

"Well, you are overweight with this big suitcase," she said, and I knew that. "£42 pounds (money) is the extra charge," she said. I was just about to pay her when she said, "Are you all together?"

"Yes," I said.

"Well here, you take this," handing Derek a small case. "You take that one," handing Alan a bag that had all our photos of family in it. Then she handed a small carry on to Sharon and gave me two bags to carry on. Then she said, "Separate. Don't let anyone know you are all together."

"Never has there been so much carry on luggage," she smiled and pushed my money back into my wallet as I tried to pay her. "Have this one on me," she said.

## Dot Goldie

Nick and Marie saw what had happened and both praised God. "Goodbye lovey," said Nick.

"Bye da'ling," said Marie as we carried our up the gangway onto the plane.

*Was that lady another angel?* I wondered.

# The Encourager

## THE JOURNEY

The journey to Miami was about ten hours, and the kids were great. I never had a problem with them the whole trip. But, I had a problem when it came to filling out the immigration form that the airlines hand you before landing.

What was I going to put down on the paper when it asks, "Are you visiting or resident?" When the flight attendant handed me mine I prayed, "O Lord, help me fill this out honestly." So, I did! I duly answered all the questions and signed it and handed it in when they requested it, and that was the end of it. Nobody came back to me or asked me anything more about it. When we eventually landed and disembarked we were all very tired.

I prayed, "Oh, Lord, help me now to get through immigration and customs without any trouble, please." I was so nervous about our passports, so as we stood in line my heart raced. *Would the immigration officer notice it said, "No entry for the United States of America,"* or would God do as

## Dot Goldie

I had asked, and blind his eyes to it and let us go on our way? Well, I didn't have long to wait.

The officer called us forward and looked us up and down. He smiled at Sharon and then asked, "How long do you intend to stay?"

I was kind of shocked. I never thought I'd be asked question. So my answer was quite spontaneous.

"I don't know," I replied. I had no idea if they would even let me in. Never mind answering: "How long would I be staying!"

He smiled at the kids and then asked them, "Do you like the beach?"

"Yes," they all said.

"All right then, have a nice visit. Enjoy yourselves." And he let us go! He stamped our passports for nine months.

*Whew*, I sighed a sigh of relief.

We made our way through the crowd toward the carousels where we were to pick up our baggage. When we reached our designated carousel no one was around.

*Wow!* I thought to myself. This is good. Then the announcement came over the loud speakers, "Our luggage

## The Encourager

was delayed thirty minutes." We would have to wait. As we waited the place began to fill up.

*I'll never get all our things now, this crowd is impossible,* I thought. *I'm going to be here all day!*

We had collected the two guitars and Derek's Ice pick pole and Sharon's huge, stuffed St. Bernard dog from the special hold on the plane, plus we had "carry on luggage" piled against a wall.

I was getting nervous now. How was I going to handle all this and get it all on a hand cart? And how was I going to make my way through the crowd with three kids, two guitars, a huge stuffed animal and seven suitcases and bags? Suddenly, a whistling shiny-faced black man came up to us with a cart and asked, "Is this your stuff Ma'am?"

"Yes," I said, "but I've got more luggage to collect from the carousel!"

"Okay, ma'am, you stay with the little girl and the boys can show me your suitcases that have to be picked up."

He was such a "God send."

He and the boys went to get the bags and I sat with Sharon and the guitars, dog and the rest of the stuff. They soon returned and the man stacked everything neatly onto this narrow long cart. I don't know how he managed it but he did!

"Follow me!" He said, and I thought, *that's what Jesus says, "Follow Me!"* So we did, and to my amazement he took us straight up to what I thought was an empty customs booth, but as we neared it a customs officer walked into the booth.

"Do you have anyone meeting us?" The nice black man asked us.

"Yes, my husband Jim will be here to get us," I said, as we reached the customs officer.

"Anything to declare?"

"No," I said and at that, he put his check mark on all our stuff.

"Have a nice trip!" the officer said and we walked out. Just as we got through Jim saw us and jumped over the wall to greet us.

"Someone is pleased to see you," the black man said, as Jim embraced us with hugs and kisses. That black man disappeared and we never saw him again. To this day, I truly believe he was another angel sent by God to help us get

## The Encourager

through customs. We never waited in line and there were hundreds of people in that place all pushing and shoving each other, and we sailed through it all. Praise God.

## THE REUNION

It was such a reunion with Jim, we never noticed or cared about our suitcases. Jim was just so glad we all arrived safe and sound and was overjoyed at seeing us that he totally forgot about the bags. Jim excitedly told us about the car he had brought to pick us up, and all what he was doing, so we all piled into the car and drove off.

We stopped on the way at a Denny's to have a cup of tea and just talked and talked about what God was doing in all our lives. Eventually, we all got back in this beautiful tan colored Buick that Debbie loaned Jim to pick us up in. A voice spoke to you when you got in it, saying, "Put on your seat belt; please, close the doors."

The kids and I were tickled by it all. Jim drove us up I-95 until we got to Chris Greenman's house, where to my amazement when we approached the door, there was all our luggage! To this day, I don't know how that stuff got there,

## The Encourager

except that my whistling, smiling, shiny-faced black man was another Angel in my life, and I truly believe he delivered it there.

    We prayed and thanked God that we were at last altogether as a family once again. Never to be apart like that ever again. *Thank You, Lord.* It was great to be in America. Everyone was happy. Already we were beginning to feel that we belonged.

# Dot Goldie

## NEW COVENANT AND THE FAMILY

The church family welcomed us with open arms. Folks were eager to meet us and offer help if needed. We stayed with Chris for a few weeks until we found a place of our own, with Chris' older daughter Deb's help. She was a real estate agent and a flight attendant with Pan Am, so she found us a townhouse in Coral Springs.

She'd told us the owner did not want kids in the house but she assured him we would take good care of the property. To move in, he also required $650 a month for rent with first, last and security. She told him we couldn't afford to pay that much and talked him into renting it to us for $500 a month and we would cut the grass. She made the deal and we moved in.

The folks at church had donated bits and pieces of furniture to us and when we moved in and had the phone connected. I got a call from Ann Kozaca, a lady from the church.

## The Encourager

"Are you the folks that need furniture?" Ann asked.

"Yes," I said.

"Can you come over to Lighthouse Point, my mother-in-law died three months ago and we need to empty her condo over here! Come and take what you need or want."

We were flabbergasted.

*Does God know our need or what?* Holly came with her VW van. I got a car given to me by Al Gritter, a car dealer. It was a hatch back and Jim had the Toyota that Pam gave him, plus Chris had her car and we did several runs loading up all the goodies. We got a dining set, a couch, two easy chairs, toaster oven, two vacuum cleaners, dishes, silverware, end tables, lamps, coffee tables, sheets, blankets, pillows, bedspreads, table linens, towels, hangers, ironing board, iron, pots and pans, a broom and dust pan, coffee pots, kettle, tea pot, kitchen knives, everything, including toilet brushes!

The house was furnished from top to bottom and believe it or not, it all matched and I felt like I was living in a palace. This was our home now, and for the first time in five years we were back, as a small close-knit family. Oh, it felt so good! We stayed in that house for seven years. The owner

## Dot Goldie

never raised the rent in all that time, and we never met him once. He lived in New York. He trusted us with his home and we took exceptional care of it the whole time. We did meet his parents once. They owned the other side of the duplex, and they wished they had renters like us.

But that's not all the miracles that God did for us.

**The Encourager**

## THE CAR

Let me tell you a little story about that car I mentioned, the hatchback that Al Gritter gave to me. Al was an elder in our church and one evening he approached me and asked if I could drive.

"Yes, I can," I told him.

"Do you have a Florida license?" He asked.

"No, I don't," I said.

"You need to get one, but first you need a car of your own," Al said. "Here in Florida a car is not a luxury; it's a necessity. So you come down to my car dealership and we will fit you with a car. I'll put blocks on the pedals so you can reach them!" He said, laughing.

I was flabbergasted. He was giving me a car. Then that familiar small voice in my head said, "Remember I told you. I will multiply back to you in this lifetime.'" And also the words, *Double Portion* ran in my mind. God gave us two-fold!

*Wow! How awesome is that?* Al told me I could use the

car until we could afford to buy something else later on.

A few months passed and Al came back to us and said that he and Pastor George Callahan had been talking together about our situation.

"You have to establish a credit line and we both will go as guarantors for you," said Al. "I have this nice little Datsun station wagon that I will fix up for you and we will take you to the bank and you can take out a loan and that way you will establish a good line of credit."

So we did that. Both George and Al signed papers saying if we defaulted they would pay the balance of the loan. Praise God, they did not have to do that. We were able to pay it all back ourselves and thus established our credit. We never realized that that would be something we would need. To this day our credit rating is A+.

*What was God up to? Where would He lead us next?* He would answer that question soon enough.

Some time went by since God gave me that car. One day Jim was doing some carpentry work for our friend Gay at her house.

## The Encourager

"I need a cleaner," she said suddenly.

"Maybe Dot can help," he told her.

I did help her, and as it turned out it proved to be an opening for me to start my own wee cleaning business. Gay told her friends that I was a Christian, that I did good work and that if they wanted a cleaner, I was it! Little did we know how God would use this little cleaning business.

I had opportunity to share my faith with all of my clients, many of whom were non-Christians when I first met them, but at the right time, they accepted the Lord Jesus as their Savior.

It was during those years that God began to speak to us about going on the missions field. Every time we heard a message about missions, our hearts were stir  Just like the Lord had done in Scotland at that conference, here we were, over a decade later, anticipating God's next move for us. When our pastor told us he was going to Bogata, Colombia, we knew God had given us our next assignment.We raised the money and went, just as the Lord told us to do.

# Dot Goldie

## THE MISSION FIELD
### Eduardo

Sometime in 1994, Jim and I went on our first short term missions trip to Bogota, Colombia. Our church team was helping the local church and ministering to the pastors from other churches in Bogota and its surrounding areas.
We got an invitation to go to Bucaramanga, and that is where I met Eduardo.

Our pastor had just finished his teaching in the little room where we were meeting and he invited the people to come forward for ministry if they needed healing, counsel or salvation.

Many people came forward and we, the team, ministered to all who came. The little living room was packed with people and some were sitting on the stairs that led up to other rooms above us. It was there on the bottom step I noticed Eduardo, a young good looking with black hair and dark eyes teenage boy. He was dressed all in black.

## The Encourager

Black jeans, black shirt, black denim jacket and black shoes. His long black hair was tied back in a ponytail. He just sat and watched all that was going on in the room. He had come with three teenage girls to the meeting.

Eduardo watched intensely as each of the girls he came with accepted Jesus as their Savior. He looked as though he wanted to get out, but couldn't because of all the people. I felt the prompting of the Spirit in my heart to go speak with him.

At first, I was hesitant, as I don't speak Spanish very well, but the urging inside me got stronger and I thought my heart would explode inside me if I didn't go speak to him.

So I motioned to Christina, my interpreter, and asked her to interpret for me. Of course she was thrilled to do this, as she is an evangelist at heart herself. So we made our way across the room to the stairs where Eduardo was now standing.

"Can we pray with you?" We asked him. He shook his head. Not interested. Then we spoke to him about the girls he had come with. "Jesus has changed their lives," we said.

"They will no longer be the same as they were when

they came in." We explained that Jesus had come into their lives and made them new creatures in Him.

"Do you want to do that?" I asked him. "Do you want to invite Jesus into your life?"

"*Si*," he said, yes, he would. "But not here, with all these people watching." So I asked the boy who led the worship if there was another room we could use to minister to Eduardo. He told me we could use his room upstairs. He lived in the house. So all four of us went upstairs. At first Eduardo was a bit awkward about "this stuff."

"Just relax," I reassured him through Christina. "Close your eyes and hold out your hands as if you were receiving a gift." He did this, and I began to pray over him.

All of a sudden, he began to twist and bend his body backwards and then straightening himself upright, with his eyes closed all the while. Then it was as though the Lord spoke to me and said, "Take off that necklace that's around his neck!"

I looked at him and saw he was wearing some kind of stone on a black leather lace around his neck. "I'm going to remove that necklace," I said as I reached over to him.

## The Encourager

He never opened his eyes the whole time, neither did he object to me removing the necklace. As soon as I removed the necklace, he began to twist and move his body until he was on the floor. I knew something demonic was going on so we earnestly prayed for Jesus to deliver him from whatever bondage Satan had over him.

About thirty minutes or so later, he was totally set free. When he was able to finally talk to us.

"Satan wanted me to run from this place, but every time I tried, I heard your voice just saying, 'Jesus, help him. Jesus set him free.'"

The name of Jesus was what kept him and set him free. He was totally changed. The darkness was gone from his eyes and the smile on his face was incredible. Jesus came into his life that night.

His parents came to church the next day and told us they hardly recognized their own son, that he was so different and that they too wanted to accept Jesus into their lives. The whole family got saved that day. All because I took the time and listened to the Holy Spirit's prompting. Praise God.

## Dot Goldie

### THE WOMAN FROM BOGOTA

One evening at the Bogota Church, my husband Jim was praying for some people that had come forward for ministry. We usually pray together as a team, but this night there were so many needs that we split up to pray for as many people as we could. I was just a couple of feet away from Jim when this incident happened.

Jim was about to anoint this lady with oil, as the Bible says to do in the book of James, when suddenly she pushed his hand away.

"I'm only anointing you with oil before praying for you," he explained through his interpreter. But, as he went to anoint her head again, she pushed his hand down, again. It was then that Jim knew something else was going on, so he called me to come over to minister alongside him, thinking maybe she wanted a woman to pray with her. So I went over and before I even prayed with her I laid my hand on her shoulder and she pushed me away!

## The Encourager

I knew then that this was not going to be dealt with at the front of the church. So, I called over to a pastor to come over beside us. He came over and we explained what had happened. So he prayed for her and she never pushed his hand away. "There, she's OK now," He said after he finished praying for her. I reached out to hug her and immediately she pushed me away.

"Don't touch me! Don't touch me!" She yelled at me, and the pastor immediately recognized that more ministry was needed. He called the leaders of the church and asked if we could take this woman up to an office or room away from the congregation to minister to her.

They immediately made the pastor's office available for our use. Six of our team members, along with the church pastor and his assistant, went into the office to pray with this woman.

"We are going to pray for your deliverance," we told her, as we sat her down in a chair. She agreed, so we began to pray. We all stood around her and laid hands on her.

Our pastor sat in front of her and held her hand. I was behind her and had both my hands on her back. Then as we ministered to her, the demonic manifestations began. She kicked at those in front of her, and the pastor and his chair fell sideways. In the meantime, I'm leaning over her from behind trying to hold her down. My arms were fully outstretched across her body; I was practically lying on top of her.

"Come out in the name of Jesus Christ," I heard myself saying in a loud voice as I held her. I repeated this over and over, and suddenly I felt something else was happening in me! I felt as though someone was on top of me holding her down also. It was a very intense moment. Everyone had let her go, except me, as I repeated, "Come out of her, in Jesus' name."

The demons finally left her. She was free at last.

Her husband came up to the room minutes later and said that she looked different. She was so happy. She was free.

That evening in church our pastor had a rededication of marriage vows, and this lady and her husband renewed theirs. Both of them were extremely grateful to God for all He had done. *Praise God!*

## The Encourager

Later that night, as Jim and I were going to bed, I couldn't stop thinking about the feeling I had had when I was holding that woman down.

"I think it was Jesus in me helping me control that lady, because no one else had a hand on her after she kicked and screamed at the pastor," I said, and that thought stuck with me for many years. I mean, we were in a tight space and when the demons manifested themselves everyone let go, except me. And I was the smallest among all of the team that was there. It must have been Jesus; because there's no way that I could have held her down in my own strength. Later on, we praised God for His presence with us and for His grace and mercy.

When I woke up the next day the muscles in my forearms were sore. But it was worth it all to see that lady set free by the power of Jesus' name. Amen!

## Dot Goldie

## AFRICA

I went to Abidjan on the Ivory Coast, where our team was sent to minister at a conference there. One night we had an altar call for salvation first then for healing. The American team was asked to come forward to pray for the sick, so I went up to the front, then the people were invited to come. I was nervous and excited at the same time.

*Lord, let me pray for headaches or stomachs*, I prayed, because I saw these two women coming toward me for prayer, and one of them was blind.

*Oh, no Lord, let them go to somebody else to pray for them,* I prayed, but I think I knew God's answer when I saw the women coming toward my French interpreter, a man from Toga, and me. The woman leading the blind lady virtually pushed her in front of me.

"Pray. Pray () in French," she said. So I began to pray in English at first then in the Spirit (tongues), a gift of the Holy Spirit. Nothing happened. Eventually some other

## The Encourager

team members came alongside of me and they prayed. Still nothing. In the meantime, crippled people were being healed all around me. They came on pallets and got up and walked. Healing was going on all over the place, it was amazing, but this woman was still blind.

"The lady has demons and she wants deliverance," my interpreter told me. And just as he said that my attention turned to a little baby that was healed, and I began praising God for his healing. Then just as I was about to pray again for my blind lady, the interpreter tapped my shoulder.

"Madam, she can see!" He said, and I jumped up and down shouting, "Praise God! She can see! She can see!" I was thrilled and overjoyed that I didn't give up on her, even though I very nearly did.

Other people had prayed over my lady and had moved on to pray with others when nothing was happening with her, but I couldn't get away from her. It was as though the Lord Himself restrained me and taught me a lesson.

Later that night I teamed up with J. B. McCoy, one of our team members. He spoke French fluently and did a lot of interpreting for the pastors when they preached

## Dot Goldie

from the pulpit. We both found ourselves walking around the perimeter of the field where 20,000 people were in attendance, and all the ministry was taking place.

Suddenly, we came across five men holding down this giant of a woman who was demon possessed. There's a lot of that in Africa. The men called out to us for help.

"Pree'a Pree'a in French," J. B. said to me. "They want you to pray for her."

"OK," I said.

"Tell her to hold her chin," the men directed, turning to me. "The demons… they bite!" So I held her chin and began to pray in the Spirit and in English for this woman's deliverance. Suddenly, the five men who were having a difficult time holding her down relaxed their hold on her, and the woman lay motionless on the red sandy dirt.

At first I thought she was dead. Then she slowly began to move and get up. When she stood up straight, she was a giant of a woman. She motioned towards me.

I thought, *Oh, no, she's going to crush me!* But she was all smiles and pulled me toward her. My head was at the height of her belly.

## **The Encourager**

She repeated over and over, *"Merci beaucoup, merci beaucoup, merci beaucoup,"* which meant, "Thank you very much, thank you very much, thank you very much."

Once again, the Lord set another child free to worship Him. J. B. and I had a lot to talk about later in the evening, and we both sang and worshipped God the rest of the night.

# Dot Goldie

## INDIA

A few years later, Jim and I went to India with a medical team after the 2004 Indian Ocean earthquake and tsunami hit. It's recorded that altogether, an estimated 230,000 to 260,000 people died. The quake itself was the third-most powerful since 1900, exceeded only by the Great Chilean Earthquake of 1960 (magnitude 9.5), and the 1964 Good Friday Earthquake in Prince William Sound, Alaska (magnitude 9.2); both of those quakes also produced killer tsunamis in the Pacific Ocean basin but the Indian Ocean tsunami was the most deadly in recorded history.

Jim and I were counselors on the team that was sent to Pondicherry, a place by the ocean that was completely wiped out by the tsunami.

We worked with another team from Operation Mobilization (O.M.), a wonderful organization, working worldwide, serving the Lord as missionaries. We all had an interpreter, as the language spoken where we were was

## The Encourager

Tamil. God gave us Suganthi and Uma, two wonderful "Dalit" girls as interpreters, as they were fluent in English and Tamil.

The Dalit caste in India is the lowest caste of all. They are treated like slaves. Dogs are more highly thought of than a "Dalit." It's awful how they are treated; they can't even worship in the Hindu Temple, even though they are Hindu.

It's terrible! They are the poorest of the poor; the ones who deal with the dead animals or dead people. They are seen as unclean, like the lepers in the Bible, and our team was in India to minister to them.

The Dalits were delighted that we had come to help them—the survivors. Jim and I heard many sad stories during that time we were there, but our awesome God showed up powerfully and through the ministry of the medical team and us as counselors. We saw many come into the kingdom, and many were healed also.

An old gentleman, a Hindu came into our tent for counseling. He told me his story of how he survived the tsunami and ended up in hospital with broken limbs, etc.

"I had a dream one night that Jesus came into my room and stood at the foot of my bed," he said.

## Dot Goldie

"He offered me a liter of water then moved to the man in the bed next to me and gave him two liters of water. I want to know why did I only get one liter and the other man got two?"

Right away the Lord spoke to my heart and said, "Tell him I'm I AM, the living water and I want to come live inside him. I am the only true Living God and that if he drinks of Me, the living water, he will never thirst again. Tell him the other man who got two liters of water worships other gods and he will thirst again. But tell him I have come to him to live in him and desire to give him eternal life that he might live with Me and Me with him."

So, I asked the man, "Do you want Jesus, who is the Living Water, to come live inside you?"

"Yes, yes, I want this Living Water in me," he said. I led him in the prayer of salvation and he left our tent rejoicing. I also gave him a bottle of water to take home with him, as drinking water in these parts was very scarce, and for Dalits very expensive. So he was doubly happy, and we thanked God for His Word.

# The Encourager

## THE 110 YEAR OLD WOMAN

One hundred and ten years old. That was how old this precious Dalit woman was. She was all shook up by the tsunami, a series of four enormous waves that had crashed ashore, the highest recorded at 24 meters tall (80 feet).

Once the waves hit the shallows, in some places the local geography channeled them into even larger monsters, as much as 30 meters (100 feet) tall. This woman had seen her whole family wiped out. Her daughter and husband, and her grand children were all gone and only she was left.

"Why did God leave me?" She cried as tears ran down her wrinkled cheeks. "Why did He not kill me?" she wailed.

"I'm old, they were all young!" She wept. Finally, I asked her about her story of the tsunami. She told me that all her family was Christians, but that she was still Hindu. She had a good business and a beautiful home, but she lost everything and everyone that was precious to her. Now she

## Dot Goldie

was living in a shack with no money, no friends, and no family. She was sick because she had swallowed so much water during the tsunami. Her body was hurting all over, and though she had no broken bones, they were all bruised.

She was mad at God for losing her home, money and family... in that order.

"Tell me about your family," I asked her. "They all left the temple and Hindu religion," she said. "They found another religion called Christianity. I was afraid to leave the temple to go with them, because they would not allow her to get food and water if I turned to the Christians."

"So fear kept you back," I said. And she nodded.

"My daughter talked to me about Jesus, but I did not want to hear about Him. I can be killed if I become a Christian," she said. So, she would just worship her gods and keep her house and business. Then, the tsunami struck and took it all away. Her house, I think, was the most dear to her of all. She seemed so proud of what she had.

I spoke to her from John's Gospel, Chapter 14, where Jesus speaks of building us a house—a mansion, in fact, in Heaven.

## The Encourager

"God has spared your life to give you another opportunity to accept Him, as your Lord and Savior," I told her. "Your family is now enjoying eternal life with Jesus and they no longer have to worry about anyone killing them or having to look for drinking water, as they are now in His Presence healed, restored and living well."

"Jesus is also building me a house that one day I too would be with Him," I explained. "I will also meet your daughter and son-in-law and your grand children when I arrive in Heaven. Who knows, they might be my next door neighbors!"

Then I said, "If you asked Jesus to be your Savior, maybe I would be your neighbor and we could have a cup of tea together," I laughed.

She laughed too but then asked, "How do I get Jesus to be my Savior?"

I shared the Word of God with her and then she gladly accepted Jesus as her Savior.

*Praise God for His wonder, working power!*

**Dot Goldie**

## NO INTERPRETER NEEDED

*God is my Translator*

Counseling is wonderful when all concerned speak the same language. During our trip to India we always had Suganthi or Uma to translate for us whenever we had a counselee. This one morning, however, Jim and his translator were out somewhere else in the camp.

I was left in the counseling tent with Suganthi. Well, nature called and Suganthi had to go to the restroom, which was on the other side of the camp.

"Will you be alright on your own until I come back?" she said.

"Of course, I'll be fine," I said, and so off she went.

She was no sooner gone when this dear old woman came into my tent. It was obvious that she was in a lot of pain. I greeted her saying, "Vanacume," with my hands folded in prayer position. That's how the Indians greet one another. She was delighted with this greeting, and I must have said it

## The Encourager

well because she immediately began to speak in Tamil, her native tongue. I tried to tell her that I didn't understand, but I would pray for her anyway. She sat down as I motioned to her and pulled a chair over. I spoke to her in English, knowing full well she didn't understand a word I said, but pressed on.

*Lord, please,* I prayed. *Reveal to her through the Spirit what I am saying.*

I laid my hands on her, closed my eyes, and began to pray for her healing, wherever she hurt, whatever was wrong with her. The Lord knew, so I just asked Him to give her whatever it was that she needed.

*Lord, I pray for her salvation,* I prayed. *Holy Spirit please interpret for me that she might know her need of the Savior, and for her to accept Him into her life, that she would know Him in a personal way and would forsake all her other gods that she as a Hindu worships and would only worship You, Jesus, You alone—no other but You, Jesus.*

And just as I closed that prayer in Jesus' name, Suganthi returned. Before I could say anything, the old lady started talking a mile a minute to Suganthi. I had no idea what was being said. They both talked back and forth for a moment. Suganthi was asking her some questions, then when she was satisfied with the answers she turned to me.

"She (the old lady) knows what you said to her," Suganthi said. "She said Jesus spoke to her while you were praying over her, and she says she wants to worship ONLY JESUS ALONE."

I got so excited, I just about squeezed the breath out of the old lady.

Suganthi lead her in the prayer for salvation in Tamil, and the old woman got saved! She smiled at me and laid her hands on me and just kept saying, "Jesus, Jesus, Jesus," as she patted me on the chest over and over, full of joy. That was a special day for me. *God was my translator.*

# The Encourager

## THE FIVE WOMEN

Once again I was in the counseling tent on my own. Everyone else was taking a break. We were just about finished for the day, and the men were breaking down the camp. y, so the medical tent had been taken down and all medicines were packed and stored away.

So there I was relaxing and cooling myself down with some cold water. I poured some water into my hat and as I was putting it back on my head, Chantelle, one of the women in our team, came over with five Hindu women.

This was Chantelle's first mission trip, and she hadn't seen anything like this before. These five ladies were sick but she couldn't get any meds because everything was packed up and in the truck.

"I've brought them to you to pray for them!" said Chantelle and so I put out five chairs for them to sit on. At that moment, Suganthi arrived back.

"Translate for me," I said and she nodded joyfully.

## Dot Goldie

"You are going to pray too," I told Chantelle, and she nodded. "I have no special powers, so Jesus can hear your prayers, as well as mine." She nodded again.

The chairs were in a circle. I stood in the middle, with Suganthi moving from one lady to another praying silently over them. While I was praying, I laid hands on them in Jesus' Name, asking Him to heal their wounds from the tsunami, to heal their minds and take away the horror of all they had been through and for them to receive His Peace that passes all understanding, and that He be glorified in all their lives.

"Jesus, you are their healer. You are the GREAT PHYSICIAN of us all... Hallelujah! Hallelujah!" I prayed. Some of the other team members heard us and leaned over the curtain that separated us.

"What's going on over there?" They said smilingly.

"We want some of it." In no time, we were all filled with the joy of the Lord. The ladies accepted Jesus as their Lord and Savior and I sent them away telling them to thank Jesus, as they walked back to their huts.

"I pray Jesus goes with you," I told them. "He will never leave you or forsake you." They all went away arm in

## The Encourager

arm, walking back to the village. It had been a wonderful time. Chantelle was beaming.

"I knew this was a good idea!" She said. "I couldn't let them go without getting at least a prayer." We all agreed. About ten minutes later the five women came back to my tent with five more ladies!

"They want you to pray with them for Jesus to come into their lives," Suganthi told me. I was overcome with sheer joy and welcomed the women in and sat them down in a circle, and went through the same things as before, and they all accepted Jesus and went home giving God the Glory, and so did I.

## Dot Goldie

## THE $6,000 GIFT

We had been in Florida for seven years, when we received a letter from U.S. Immigration to say that we had an interview to become "Legal Aliens." The thing was, we had to fly to London, and so, what should have been one of the happiest days of our lives was marred by one very important thing. MONEY. We only had twenty-six dollars to our name, and we needed to fly back to London in a couple of weeks.

*What do we do now, Lord?* We prayed. At that time, I had been leading the worship at church in the six o'clock prayer meeting every morning for several years previously. So naturally I asked for prayer from the guys that attended that early morning prayer time.

Then when I got the news about going back to London, the pastor, who knew our situation, asked me, "How are you going to pay for your trip?"

"Probably, we'll pay for it with the credit card and pay it off a bit at a time," I replied.

## The Encourager

"Some folks here want to help you," he said. I was astounded.

"Next Sunday evening we will take up a one time love offering to help you get your immigration papers," he said.

The next Monday morning, Nancy King, the pastor's secretary, came around to our house and with tears in her eyes, handed me a check for 6,000 dollars! I was overwhelmed. Never in a million years would I have expected anything like that.

We were all filled with joy and thanksgiving for such provision as this.

*God, You are so awesome!*

## Dot Goldie

## MONEY IS NO OBJECT TO THE LORD

As you have previously read in this book, money is not a problem for the Lord, as *"He owns the cattle on a thousand hills."* In our many times of need, our Heavenly Father has always provided.

I remember one time. We were down to our last penny, again, and we needed to put gas in our car but we didn't have enough money. Things were pretty tight. Jim was working for himself at the time and was doing a job for a friend, building furniture out of our garage. This particular day was quite frustrating because Jim had to put some of the things he was building out in the driveway in order to make room inside the garage where he was working.

Well, I was at work and my car wouldn't start so I had called Jim to come help me. My job was only a couple of miles away from the house, so he decided to leave the stuff out in the driveway, as it would take only a few minutes for him to pick me up and bring me home. Living in Florida during the

## The Encourager

summer you never know when you will get a shower of rain. And that's what happened when Jim came to get me. When we got back to the house, all the stuff on the driveway was soaked. Jim was so upset because he thought it would all be ruined and our friend had already paid for everything up front.

"How are we going to fix this?" He said. "We've got no money to buy more wood. What a mess!" He was so upset.

"It's all going to be twisted," he kept saying. "It got wet with the rain... it will fall apart ." I felt so bad for him. He had worked so hard and long on that project and he is such a perfectionist!

I really didn't know what to say to him. So, I went upstairs to our bedroom and laid down on the floor prostrate before the Lord and prayed that God would straighten out any wood that was twisted, that He would stick it together in a way that no one could pull it apart.

*Lord, go back to that tree where the wood came from, and give it back to Jim so that he can just put it all together*, I prayed. *Lord, please, I pray that there will be no need to have to buy more wood...*

## Dot Goldie

All the while I was praying I could hear Jim banging things around downstairs in the garage below me.

*Lord, please, give my husband peace of mind*, I prayed for Jim. *Please, Lord, have him trust you to make it right.*

While I was praying I reminded God about why we came to America in the first place. *Lord, we came here to go to church to be a witness and give You glory, but Oh, Lord, now we can't go because we've no money to buy gas!*

It was at that moment God spoke to my heart and said, "I've done what you've asked. The wood is straight and nothing on earth can pull it apart." Then He said, "Go to the mailbox!" as clear as day.

I got up immediately, went downstairs and out the front door. Jim was in the driveway with a level in his hand.

"What are you doing?" I asked.

"I'm trying to take this apart and put it together again to make sure it won't separate and to make it level."

"Did you check if it's level yet? Because I asked God to make it straight and besides, you won't be able to take it apart because God has fixed it for you."

He looked at me as though I had lost my marbles. I

## The Encourager

said again, "You're wasting your time trying to pull it apart." Finally, he gave up trying and put the level on the piece of furniture and to his amazement it was dead straight. "Where are you going?" He asked me.

"To the mailbox," I said.

"I already got the mail," he replied.

"Well, God just told me to go to the mailbox, so I'm going!"

I opened the mailbox and inside was an envelope. No name on it. I opened it and inside was a little square of tissue paper and a ten-dollar bill.

Gas money.

"We can go to church tonight!" I shouted as I ran up the driveway to where Jim was working.

"Where did that come from?" He asked.

"God," I said with a big smile.

"What?"

"God," I said again. He sent it. He knows our need, and we need to go to church. So, He sent gas money."

I've never found out to this day where that money came from, except that my Heavenly Father knows all my needs. And, by the way, the furniture that got soaked, stayed together and the friend that Jim made it for was so delighted with it, he offered us a weekend at his house in the Keys, where Jim installed the furniture he made.

It was a glorious St. Patrick's Day weekend. *Praise God from Whom all blessings flow.*

We also had a great time that night at church. We gave testimony as to how God met us in our time of trouble and need.

## The Encourager

## AUSTRIA

*Why Wait?* God hears and knows our need. That truth has been evident many times in my life. One day, Jim and I were discussing our future.

*What would we do when we retire?* We thought, and that question led us to talk about perhaps moving to North Carolina. And why not? We love the mountains. We discussed the possibility of serving in missions and go to different places on short term missions, as we had done previously, only this time we could stay longer as we wouldn't have to come back to a nine-to-five type of job.

We talked and talked, and the more we did missions kept coming to the fore. And then, God interrupted our conversation and said, "Why wait? Do it now!"

So we began to pray that if we got accepted to go with the team to Austria that year we would pursue the mission field and see what doors would open for us.

We got accepted for the team. We raised our support and we set off for a week of service working at the castle, which is owned by Calvary Chapel Costa Mesa. Missionaries from all Calvary Chapels all over Europe come to this castle for some rest and relaxation. Calvary Chapel Fort Lauderdale sends a team to serve in the kitchen, and other teams from Costa Mesa to do housekeeping, so missionaries can have a nice rest and enjoy the teachings and fellowship.

Before we went, we talked with Kelly Lyon, our missions pastor at the time, and shared with him that we hoped to hear from God about our future in missions. He was very encouraging and told us there would be opportunities to talk with the missionaries and we could hear from them where the needs were. So, we set off and were ready to hear, and hear we did!

During our time there we spoke with several folks and we had one special appointment with Phil and Joy Metzger, who run the Bible College in Vajta, Hungary. We had dinner with them one evening and we all just clicked.

We shared with them and they were really thrilled that an "older couple" like ourselves were willing to leave all and serve the Lord at this time in our lives.

Lisa Collins, also a missionary at the college, told us

## The Encourager

they had been praying for two years for an "older couple" to come alongside them to minister to the students that come to the college, as well as to the missionaries that staff the college. When they found out our gifts were counseling, encouragement, hospitality, evangelism and teaching small groups, they were ecstatic.

"You will fit right in!" Phil said.

We met several of the others that work at the college and all of them said, "When are you coming?"

We were filled with joy that we "fit" with these young missionaries and that they would actually want people like us to come alongside them. So, we met with Kelly again and told him all that Phil had suggested.

The plan was to go sometime in October when the college was up and running and for us to see if indeed that was what God wanted, and if so, then they would want us.

"Do you have EU passports?" Asked Phil.

"Yes, we do, but we have to have them renewed," we replied.

"That would be a big plus to be able to move around Europe," he explained, so the day we got home, we filed for our new passports. While we waiting for them, we prayed that there wouldn't be a problem, as we were now U.S. citizens. We were confident though; that when God opens a door no man can shut it, as His Word says in Revelation 3.

We took our step in faith and booked our flight for September 29 to October 15, 2006, believing God would show us His will for the future. Both my boss and Jim's had given us the time off work to pursue this calling and "God willing," if all went well with our visit, we would return to the U.S. and hopefully to the missions board at Calvary Chapel Fort Lauderdale. They would be the ones giving us their blessing so that we could then begin the process of getting our support together, and sell our home and furniture, etc. and move to Hungary.

I couldn't wait to see what happened.

## ABOUT THE AUTHOR

I was born July 25, 1945 just after the war. I grew up in Glasgow, Scotland, and my childhood was full of fun, playing in the midst of the rubble that the bombing had caused. There were lots of good places to play. Our imagination ran wild, as old bombed out washhouses became our wee playing houses. School was another thing, though. I didn't like school at all, but somehow I managed to get through it.

My parents were the best! Dad was a master butcher, Mom stayed home to look after us—my sisters and brother. Mom was a homemaker and it was nice to come home to a nice fire in the fireplace and the smell of dinner cooking on the stove. You could always tell as you entered, close to

## Dot Goldie

about four o'clock in the afternoon, that dinner was on the stove in all the houses. The aroma was everywhere. But when you got to my house you could also smell the Brasso on the door handle and bell ringer, and when the door opened the smell of floor polish hit you. I used to love that smell; it was so clean.

Mom took good care of our wee room and kitchen. My sister Agnes was five years older than me and my brother Harris was five years her senior. In those days, everyone lived in small apartments. Some families bigger than ours lived in even smaller places than ours. When my sister Lily came along eight years later, we moved across the street to a two-room and kitchen apartment. Wow! It was great. On the ground floor too. No more climbing two stories up.

We eventually got an exchange and moved to Pollock, where my mom's sister Mary, and her brother George lived. My uncle lived in the same street as us. This house was huge

## The Encourager

compared to what we had previously. We now had three bedrooms, a bathroom inside the house, and a living room and a big kitchen where we could sit down at a table and eat. It was great. We had a back and front door, and a garden in front and a garden in back. What living! We got a poodle named Tara, and he was the icing on the cake for me. We lived in that house until all three of us older kids got married. Lily stayed with mom and dad until they moved again. Then finally she too married.

    I met my husband Jim through a boy that worked for my dad. We were 15 and 16 years old. Jim is one year older than I. I was 16 1/2 when we got engaged and found a wee room and kitchen with a box room, which we made into a little eat-in breakfast room.

    We had an inside toilet, no bath, just a toilet. We went to our parents' houses to get a bath once a week. We fixed that little place up before we got married. It was beautiful.

## Dot Goldie

After our wedding, we moved in and I thought it couldn't get any better than this. Well, it did.

I eventually got pregnant and had a son Derek. He was the cutest! Then a few months later we moved to a great house with a bathroom and back and front garden. Then, I had a second son Alan. Boy, was he good looking.

Six years later, the light of my life was born. Sharon, all nine pounds of her. We were now complete. Two boys and one girl. I was convinced things could not get better than this. How wrong can a person be!

www.ingramcontent.com/pod-product-compliance
Lightning Source LLC
Chambersburg PA
CBHW061648040426
42446CB00010B/1643